The Essence of God

The Essence of God

Homilies from the Pulpit

Pastor Dr. Gloria Taylor-Boyce

Copyright © 2018 Dr. Gloria Taylor-Boyce

All rights reserved.

ISBN: 1986075354
ISBN-13: 978-1986075350

DEDICATION

To all the members of Saint Zoe Parish Church and those who welcome me into their homes during our Sunday night live conference calls

Prophet Word:
This is your season of Wisdom, Enlightenment and Divine favour.
Saith the word of the Lord.
Pastor Gloria Taylor-Boyce

Contents

PREFACE ix

CHAPTER 1 1

   WHAT ARE YOU BINDING TO YOURSELF? 1

CHAPTER 2 13

   WE DEMONSTRATE OUR MENTAL EQUIVALENT 13

CHAPTER 3 25

   VENGEANCE DAY 25

CHAPTER 4 39

   WHY TEMPT YE ME, YE HYPOCRITES? 39

CHAPTER 5 49

   IS THINE EYE EVIL, BECAUSE I AM GOOD 49

CHAPTER 6 61

   EVERY SCRIPTURE WAS INSPIRED BY GOD 61

CHAPTER 7 75

   THE GREAT AWAKENING 75

CHAPTER 8 89

- JESUS SAID TO THEM, COME WITH ME! 89
- CHAPTER 9 99
  - ABUNDANCE IS YOUR INHERITANCE 99
- CHAPTER 10 127
  - CLAIM YOUR TRUTH 127
- AFFIRMATION: 161
- CHAPTER 11 163
  - THERE IS NONE OF THY KINDRED THAT IS LED BY THIS NAME 163
- CHAPTER 12 177
  - THE GREAT COMMISSION 177
- ABOUT SAINT ZOE PARISH CHURCH 189
  - SUNDAY WORSHIP MASS / SERVICE 190
  - LOCAL WEEKLY CHURCH SERVICES 191
  - OTHER METHODS TO CONNECT: 192
- NOTES 194

PREFACE

Masterfully crafted from the teachings and wisdom of Pastor Dr. Gloria Taylor-Boyce, "**The Essence of God: *Homilies from the Pulpit***" helps readers remove the barriers, inferiority, and limitations between them and a life of plenty. Pastor Taylor-Boyce's first goal is to get readers back in control of their own thoughts and then, after helping them understand why they can live their dreams, assists them to kick-start a powerful journey of organizing their thoughts to guarantee positive results.

If there's one universal plague in humanity, it's the crippling and self-limiting belief that a life of plenty and prosperity is reserved for "other people" other than one's self.

As a passionate and dedicated Pastor, Dr. Gloria Taylor-Boyce has seen this mindset embedded into every facet of society. However, though her powerful new book **The Essence of God:** *Homilies from the Pulpit*, Pastor Taylor-Boyce is out to prove that people can have *anything* they want in life.

The Essence of God: *Homilies from the Pulpit* calls on foundational principles of the Christian faith to lay out a proven blueprint to afford each and every reader the cornucopia they have been searching for their entire lives. All it requires is an unshakable belief in God, a few simple thought adjustments and enough brevity to embark on a new life with gusto.

The Essence of God: *Homilies from the Pulpit* gives us the passion for a new possibility along with precise and clear directions for building a new way of thinking and manifestation. It shows us how to activate constructive thought and how to hold it through feeling and intention.

Everybody knows the phrase "bad things happen to good people" and, while that could be true to some extent, the absolute truth is that the solution often lies just beyond the problem, but people are too wrapped up in the negative to see it," explains Pastor Taylor-Boyce. "This book is about seeing the solution by stepping back, shifting consciousness and not taking anything personally. Nobody knows what is in your world, and you don't have to agree with their negativity toward you." The best thing is that the entire book is presented as a "wash, rinse and repeat" system;

something that can be replicated as many times as necessary throughout life, when you catch curveballs.

It's time to get back in the driver's seat and realize that you not only can live your dreams, but you deserve to.

THE ESSENCE OF GOD: Homilies from the Pulpit

CHAPTER 1
WHAT ARE YOU BINDING TO YOURSELF?

And Jesus answered and said unto him, Blessed art thou, Simon Barjona: for flesh and blood hath not revealed it unto thee, but my Father which is in heaven.18 And I say also unto thee, That thou art Peter, and upon this rock I will build my church; and the gates of hell shall not prevail against it. And I will give unto thee the keys of the kingdom of heaven: and whatsoever thou shalt bind on earth shall be bound in heaven: and whatsoever thou shalt loose on earth shall be loosed in heaven. Matthew16: 17-19

We all look forward to the day when we can truly understand who we are and not what the world brand us to be for no one can see inside you but you. In Matthew 16:13-20 we see Jesus coming into the coasts of Caesarea Philippi, and he asked his disciples, saying, *"whom do men say that I the Son of man am"?* Then in verse 16: And Simon Peter answered and said Thou art the Christ, the Son of the living God. Then in verse 19: *And I will give unto thee the keys of the kingdom of heaven: and whatsoever thou shalt bind on earth shall be bound in heaven: and whatsoever thou shalt loose on earth shall be loosed in heaven*

In an effort to identify who we are we must be aware of what are we binding to ourselves. For years I will hear many good God-fearing Christian say I bind that in the name of Jesus and the **THAT** they were referring too were never anything good. I could never understand why anyone would bind something to themselves that they definitely detest.

So today let us take a deeper look at the scripture in Matthew 18:18 Jesus said, *"Whatever you bind on earth will be bound in heaven, and whatever you loose on earth will be loosed in heaven."* Some people today claim that Jesus was telling us that we have the power to "bind" the devil and his demons. Others claim that he was talking about "binding" sickness and poverty and "loosing" health and wealth.

Today we are going to have a different approach: for we here at Saint Zoe Parish Church know that what you fight you ignite: as a result we understand that evil can touch only that person who is entertaining it; therefore we never fear evil; we never hate it; we never resent it, but always we respond with compassion.

Having said that know this! We understand that the pressures of the world not only would separate us from God, but they would separate man from man, man from wife, parent from child, friend from friend, employer from employee.

The world has made us natural enemies of one another. One animal preys upon another, and the great animal, man, preys upon all other creatures.

The way of the world is separation; the way of the Christ is oneness. Isaiah caught the vision of oneness when he said: *"The wolf also shall dwell with the lamb and the leopard shall lie down with the kid; and the calf and the young lion and the fatling together.... They shall not hurt nor destroy in all my holy mountain."*

What I am leading to is this! The essential ingredient of all satisfactory relationship is love. Our love for God is made manifest in our love for man. We are not only one with God, but we are one with the children of God: with our families and relatives, with our church members; with our business associates; with our friends. When we recognize God as our neighbour, we become members of the household of God, saints in the spiritual kingdom; there is a complete surrender of self into the infinite Sea of spirit.

Know this! The good of God flows to us through all who become a part of our universe. To those who live in communion with God. Look! What I am saying is this! When the Christ has been realized, Its activity can never be impaired, impeded, delayed, or hindered. God has a way of wiping away every obstruction. Nothing can prevent His fruits from appearing in our life when its time has come. When that moment comes, the God-force will plunge it into expression, just as unstoppable as the unborn child is expelled from the womb, when its moment arrives to appear on the scene.

We know that our good comes through grace. Now! This grace will appear as normal everyday avenues or channels if we do not interfere with its operation by planning how it can be expressed. Understanding then God to be the giver of all good, we do not look to one another even for those things which constitute our human or legal rights. So what in heaven's name are we binding and loosing?

Having said all that let us get back to the scripture in an effort to discern what Jesus was implying in Matthew 18:18: Jesus said, *"Whatever you bind on earth will be bound in heaven, and whatever you loose on earth will be loosed in heaven."*

In applying this phrase to today's understanding, we must first appreciate the time and context in which the phrase was written. No doubt Jesus used this phrase for the process—**Bind and Loose**. It was not a matter of treating the Scripture lightly, "loosing" it by tossing overboard, but rather the process treated Scripture with gravity, carefully attempting to discern how it applied to actual daily living.

Any pastor who knows real people knows the need to carefully discern the scriptures as people tend to take the bible verses literally without applying the revelation of the word which comes from within. For example, some people are simply too hard on themselves—their consciences are so tender that they'll turn in a penny they've found to the Wal-Mart counter, and if they keep it, they feel like they are a thief. These people need loosing from their hard taskmaster "Themselves."

On the other hand, there are also others who are so liberal on themselves they will "loose" just about every command in

Scripture—including explicit ones—as they "consider the circumstances" in their own life. We all recently heard of the registered nurse who overdoses some elderly residents because she said the word of God told her to do so.

They'll be sinning boldly and pronouncing it good. These sorts of people could use a bit of "binding." The bottom line is individuals cannot be trusted to do their own binding and loosing—they needed a rabbi to help them, and this was the situation in the first century when Jesus spoke these words.

Rabbi Jesus did what rabbis did—they took the law and applied it to daily practical issues of morality—loosening the grip of some rules and tightening and extending others. He never disposed of the law but *applied* it to real-life through the process.

In closing I will like to say this: It is the church's job to start with God's word then look at real-life situations and decide where to bind and extend the meaning of Scripture and where to loosen up its application and turn people free.

I think it is *the church's* job to tell the person who feels guilty for the penny they stole from the parking lot that they've not stolen it at all—they should put it in the offering plate and quit fretting. The church has a moral obligation to uphold not only the word of God but moral decency as well. It is important that we never look upon the discords and in harmonies of our life as if they represented a lack of understanding or a lack of demonstrations. Regard those unfortunate circumstances as opportunities which will dissolve when they no longer serve their purpose.

Have the courage to look at every person and circumstance that you consider harmful or destructive. In the silence, face the situation fearlessly; face the condition or the person, and you will discover that it – or he – is an image of your own thoughts and, therefore, there is no cause, jurisdiction, or law to support it. Recognize God as the Soul of every person and God as the activity in every situation.

CHAPTER 2
WE DEMONSTRATE OUR MENTAL EQUIVALENT

And they went into Capernaum, and straightway on the sabbath day he entered into the synagogue, and taught. And they were astonished at his doctrine: for he taught them as one that had authority, and not as the scribes. And there was in their synagogue a man with an unclean spirit; and he cried out, Saying, Let us alone; what have we to do with thee, thou Jesus of Nazareth? art thou come to destroy us? I know thee who thou art, the Holy One of God. And Jesus rebuked him, saying, Hold thy peace, and come out of him. And when the unclean spirit had torn him, and cried with a loud voice, he came out of him. And they were all amazed, insomuch that they questioned among themselves, saying, What thing is this? What new doctrine is this? For with authority commandeth he even the unclean spirits, and they do obey him. And immediately his fame spread abroad throughout all the region round about Galilee. Mark 1:21-28

Look at this! The unclean spirit had to come out of the man. You cannot stand before Jesus all the while maintaining an unclean spirit. Much the same way anyone of us cannot invite God into our hearts while bearing grudges and resentment or carrying on a pity party. It has to come out for there was no reflection of it in Jesus. That is the law of mental equivalents: There was no embodiment in Jesus so it could not be demonstrated. *Remember everything comes after its own kind.* **WE DEMONSTRATE OUR EMBODIMENT, OUR MENTAL EQUIVALENT** or one could say our corresponding thoughts.

Now! Jesus was not just teaching He taught them as one that had authority and not as the scribes which they were observing from his outer appearance. This is the exact manner in which we must operate. We must operate as one who has authority. What I am trying to say is this if we are a real embodiment; then we will demonstrate. Look at this: If we lack, if we are poor, if we are without friends, if we are without opportunity, we should be sure to erase from our consciousness any sense of lack. We erase thought from consciousness by pouring in an opposite thought. This thought meets the other and neutralizes its effects. It rubs it out just as we rub a chalk mark off a board. We must, however, maintain a consistent, positive, aggressive mental attitude in the Truth.

Remember we walk by falling forward; water falls by its own weight; the planets are eternally falling through space; everything sustains itself in nature. The only reason man is limited is that he has not allowed the Divine within him to more completely express. Man's Divine Individuality compels Infinity to appear in his experience as duality because he has believed in duality. Let me say this! Prayer does something to the mind of the one praying. It does not do anything to God. The external gift is always made. The gift of God is the nature of God. God cannot help making the gift, because God **IS THE GIFT.** We do not have to pray for God to be God. God is God. Jesus revealed the nature of the Divine Being by his personal embodiment of the Divine Nature.

He said, *"As ye believe, it shall be done unto you."* The whole teaching of Jesus is based on the theory that we are surrounded by an intelligent Law, which does unto each as he believes. He implied the necessity of faith, conviction, and acceptance. That is, *it must be measured out to us according to our own measuring.* We must not only believe; we must know that our belief measures the extent and degree of our blessing. If our belief is limited, only a little can come to us, because that is *as we believe*. We call this law of mental equivalents. How much life can any man experience? It is determined by the amount that can be embodied by him.

There is nothing fatalistic about this. We are so constituted that we can continuously increase our embodiment. We grow in grace, as it were. We grow in power, and theoretically, there should be no limit to that growth. But right today we can expect to demonstrate or to have our prayers answered according to our belief and embodiment of that belief. It is said, *"To as many as received him, to them gave he the power."* We seek to uncover the science of prayer: the essence of the Spirit embodied in it. We find that the essence of the power of prayer is faith and acceptance. In addition to the law of faith and acceptance, the law of mental equivalents must be considered. These are the two great laws with which we have to deal, and we shall never get away from either. If prayer has been answered, it is not because God has been moved to answer one man and not another, but because one man more than another *has moved, into a right relationship* with the Spirit or the Principle of the Christ Being – whichever one chooses to call it. Faith, then, touches a Principle the Christ Being which responds, we may be certain of this. We should have more faith than we do rather than less, nor is it foolish to cultivate faith.

ALL PRAYERS WILL BE ANSWERED WHEN WE PRAY ARIGHT. The first necessity is faith. Faith! But someone may exclaim, "This is what has always been taught, this is nothing new!" Correct, we have nothing new. We simply have a new approach to an old truth, a more intelligent, and a more systematic way of consciously arriving at faith.

Why is it that Jesus could say to the paralyzed man, "Take up thy bed and walk?" Because Jesus *knew* when he said this that the man *would get up and walk.* **HE NOT ONLY BELIEVED THAT THERE WAS SOMETHING TO RESPOND TO HIM BUT HE HAD AN EQUIVALENT OF ITS RESPONSE,** which is just as necessary.

The Law is never-ending and perfect, but in order to make a demonstration, **WE MUST HAVE A MENTAL EQUIVALENT OF THE THING WE DESIRE**. A demonstration, like anything else in the objective life, is born out of a mental concept. The mind is the fashioning factor, and according to its range, vision and constructiveness will be the circumstance or experience. For example: If one sees only hate in others, it is because hate is a strong element in himself. The light he throws on others is generated in his own soul, and he sees them as he chooses to see them. He holds constantly in his mind a mental equivalent of hate and creates unlovely reactions towards himself. He is getting back what he is sending out. If a man believes himself to be a failure and that it is useless for him to try to be anything else, he carries with him the mental equivalent of failure. So he *succeeds* in being a *failure* according to law. This is his *demonstration.*

Let me tell you a story; when I was around fourteen to fifteen years of age my friend

Angela who was eighteen at the time got married and shortly after that got pregnant. I stayed with her through a very difficult birth after which I decreed that I would not have any children. That declaration came to pass as I did not give birth even after two marriages. I did however adopt.

What I'm leading to is this: Having a strong picture or mental concept, and holding to that equivalent regardless of circumstances or conditions, we must sooner or later manifest according to the concept.

It follows, then that the range of our possibilities at the present time does not extend far beyond the range of our present concept. As we bring ourselves to a greater vision, we induce a greater concept and thereby demonstrate more in our experience. In this way, there is a continuous growth taking place. We do not expect to make quantum leaps; however little by little, we can unfold our consciousness, through the acquisition of greater and still greater mental equivalents, until at last we shall be made free.

The way to proceed is to begin right where we are. One who understands the systematic use of the Law will understand that *he is where he is because of what he is*, but he will not say "I must remain where I am, because of what I am." Instead, he will begin to disclaim what appears to be. As his statements release wrong subjective tendencies, providing in their place a correct concept of life and Reality, he will automatically be lifted out of his condition; impelling forces sweeping everything before them, will set him free if he trusts in Spirit and the working of the Law.

Stay with the One the indwelling Christ and never deviate from It, never leave It for a moment. Nothing else can equal this attitude. **TO DESERT THE TRUTH IN THE HOUR OF NEED IS TO PROVE THAT WE DO NOT KNOW THE TRUTH**. When things look the worst DO NOT FRET! That is the supreme moment to demonstrate to ourselves that there are no obstructions to the operation of Truth. When things look the worst is the best time to work, the most satisfying time. The person who can throw himself with a complete abandon into that Limitless Sea of Receptivity, A sea of Openness; having cut loose from all apparent ties or knots, is the one who will always receive the greatest reward.

CHAPTER 3

VENGEANCE DAY

All things which are written may be fulfilled.

And when ye shall see Jerusalem compassed with armies, then know that the desolation thereof is nigh. Then let them which are in Judaea flee to the mountains; and let them which are in the midst of it depart out; and let not them that are in the countries enter there into. For these be the days of vengeance, that all things which are written may be fulfilled. But woe unto them that are with child, and to them that give suck, in those days! for there shall be great distress in the land, and wrath upon this people. And they shall fall by the edge of the sword, and shall be led away captive into all nations: and Jerusalem shall be trodden down of the Gentiles, until the times of the Gentiles be fulfilled. And there shall be signs in the sun, and in the moon, and in the stars; and upon the earth distress of nations, with perplexity; the sea and the waves roaring; Men's hearts failing them for fear, and for looking after those things which are coming on the earth: for the powers of heaven shall be shaken. And then shall they see the Son of man coming in a cloud with power and great glory. And when these things begin to come to pass, then look up, and lift up your heads; for your redemption draweth nigh. Luke 21:20-28

In life, we all make mistakes which in the end catch up with us. It may start off innocently like a little lie, or something you took from someone without their permission, or even trying to trick or deceive someone out of something for your own pleasure. In the end, there will always be a day of vengeance if we do not make recompense before that day arrives. We all have to make atonement for our shortcomings!

IN TODAY'S SCRIPTURE Jesus is reminding us that sometimes life deals us some devastating blows: Luke 21:20: *And when ye shall see Jerusalem compassed with armies, then know that the desolation thereof is nigh.* In real meaning, when you see soldiers camped all around Jerusalem, then you'll know that she is about to be devastated. Similarly, when things are happening around you all at once: Negative reports coming from the East, the West, the North, and the South, all trying to infiltrate your place of safety. In essence camping all around your Jerusalem. Know this! (Jerusalem is that save place in the heavens of your mind.) Now you have all these thoughts trying to mess up your equilibrium; Trying to disturb your peace:

Then we see Jesus is saying in Luke 21:21: *Then let them which are in Judaea flee to the mountains; and let them which are in the midst of it depart out; and let not them that are in the countries enter theirinto.*

In this Bible story, it should be noted that History records that no Christian lost his life in the incredible devastation that overtook Jerusalem, the certainty that they did escape being the only authentication of Jesus' prophecy that is necessary.

In like manner, you also could escape your day of vengeance if you flee to the mountains after seeing the signs. The warning here is vivid and pointed. At the first indication of approaching troops, they are to find refuge not in the city for that is doomed, but in the caves on the wild, deserted mountains. In essence, you cannot find peace in the city of your mind. You cannot find peace in the state where the disturbance resides. There must be a shifting from one house to another. In my Father's house, there are many mansions. So what is being described here is the fact that it can be avoided by fleeing to the mountains. The emphasis is on the reality that the judgment is centered on Jerusalem. One must, therefore, flea to the mountains.

Then again, we see Jesus is saying in Luke 21:22: *For these be the days of vengeance, that all things which are written may be fulfilled.* Let us not act all surprised! For we all knew that the day of reckoning would come when we have to face the consequences of our actions. *"As a man thinketh in his heart, so is he,"* not only embraces the whole of a man's being but is so comprehensive as to reach out to every condition and circumstance of his life. A man is literally what he thinks, his character being the complete sum of all his thoughts. Also, as the plant springs from and could not be without the seed, so every act of a man springs from the hidden seeds of thought and could not have appeared without them. This applies equally to those acts called "spontaneous" and "unpremeditated," as to those which are deliberately executed.

However, because we have learned certain lessons along the way, the experience does not have to be unpleasant: We must, however, get out of harm's way: How do you do that? By fleeing to the mountain: The next question is how does one flee to the mountain? You flee to the mountain by flooding your mind with the promises of God. "I will never leave you or forsake you" *"The Lord is my shepherd; I shall not want"* *"He restoreth my soul: He leadeth me in the paths of righteousness for his name's sake." "Yea, though I walk through the valley of the shadow of death, I will fear no evil: for thou art with me; thy rod and thy staff they comfort me." "Thou preparest a table before me in the presence of mine enemies: thou anointest my head with oil; my cup runneth over."* Every hour in the day, flood your mind with goodness.

We then move on to what Jesus is saying in Luke 21:23: *But woe unto them that are with child and to them that give suck, in those days! for there shall be great*

distress in the land, and wrath upon this

people. A different way of saying this is; pregnant and nursing mothers will have it especially hard. Incredible misery! Pouring rage! Here Jesus is saying those who are already facing a challenge this would be an added burden; All the more reason to get out of your head and into the word of God.

In verses Luke 21:24-26 Jesus is saying what would happen: People dropping like flies; people dragged off to prisons; Jerusalem under the boot of barbarians until the nations finish what was given them to do. Then in verse 25-26 It will seem like all hell has broken loose — sun, moon, stars, earth, sea, in an uproar and everyone all over the world in a panic, the wind knocked out of them by the threat of doom, the powers-that-be quaking.

After all this Jesus went on to say in Luke

21:28 *And when these things be* [gin]
to pass, then look up, and li[ft up your]
heads; for your redemption dra[weth nigh.]
What Jesus is saying is this! When all this starts to happen, get up on your feet. Stand tall with your heads high. Help is on the way!" *For I will never leave you or forsake you!*

I am asking you to let this day be a day of atonement for your shortcomings of the past! You don't have to try and remember them. Just say within yourself *Father God, One thing have I desired, that I might know Thee: One thing! My heart cries out, God open Yourself to me, reveal Yourself to me. I care not whether You reveal Yourself in wealth or in health, in poverty or in sickness; only reveal Thyself. In Thy Presence is security, safety, peace, and joy!*

or nothing occupies time or space but our mental images, and the reason they do, is because we accept a yesterday, a today, and a tomorrow. The minute we rise above the mental realm of life, we shall perceive that there is no such thing as time. So how do one rise above the so-call negative thoughts and images?

I will like to leave you with this activity: When these so-call negative thoughts flow through your mind do not put value on them. These images may testify to disease; they may testify to sin; they may testify to the accident, but no matter how frightening they are, we remain steadfast on the word of God unmoved and just watch them come and go.

Remember the Christ Destroys the Enemy Within: let us follow the Master for a moment into the wilderness where he was tempted. Do you see that it was the evil within himself that was tempting him and that he was saying unto evil, "Get thee behind me, Satan" I cannot be tempted, for I am not here to glorify myself, but that God may be glorified. If I perform a miracle to glorify myself, I will have lost the kingdom of God. "Get thee behind me"

Then when his consciousness was made free of personal sense, personal glorification, self-preservation, he could go forward and fulfill his ministry because now he could not be tempted by anything external to himself. He had overcome the world when the enemy within his gates had been overcome, and the enemy within his gates was the mortal sense of selfhood that sought to preserve itself, instead of wanting to let itself "die" in order that I might be exalted, that the spirit of God in him might be the light of the world.

When there was no longer any personal sense left, when the Master was no longer living his own life, he had the capacity to heal the sick, to raise the dead, to forgive the sinner, and to feed the hungry because then he knew that his finite capacities were of no importance whatsoever, and were not to be relied upon. He had no small capacities or great capacities: he had no capacities, period. He was the transparency for the divine capacity, the spiritual, the infinite, the all-capacity.

In closing let me say this! The kingdom of God is within you and me, and the function of the Christ is to purify you and me. We are not to call upon the Christ to do something to someone else, but we are to realize that the Christ is functioning in human consciousness to dispel personal sense, first in us, in our friends, and then in our enemies.

Let us pray for the enemy that we may be children of God, pray the prayer of realization that the kingdom of God be just as much in our enemy as in our friend, awaiting only this recognition to be brought up from the tomb, raised again, and resurrected into life eternal.

PASTOR DR. GLORIA TAYLOR-BOYCE

CHAPTER 4

WHY TEMPT YE ME, YE HYPOCRITES?

Then went the Pharisees, and took counsel how they might entangle him in his talk. And they sent out unto him their disciples with the Herodians, saying, Master, we know that thou art true, and teachest the way of God in truth, neither carest thou for any man: for thou regardest not the person of men. Tell us, therefore, What thinkest thou? Is it lawful to give tribute unto Caesar, or not? But Jesus perceived their wickedness, and said, Why tempt ye me, ye hypocrites? Shew me the tribute money.

And they brought unto him a penny. And he saith unto them, Whose is this image and superscription? They say unto him, Caesar's. Then saith he unto them, Render therefore unto Caesar the things which are Caesar's; and unto God the things that are God's. **Matthew 22:15-21**

In Matthew 22: 15-21 we see Jesus asking the question: Why Tempt Ye Me, Ye Hypocrites? The Pharisees wanted to see how they might entangle Jesus. Matthew 22:15 states:"*Then went the Pharisees, and took counsel how they might entangle him!* My question to you today is, Have you ever tried to entangle someone? To entangle means to "ensnare," or "trap" as birds are taken by a net. This is done secretly, by leading them within the compass of the net and then suddenly springing it over them. So to entangle is artfully to lay a plan for enticing; to charm or lure by proposing a question, and by leading, if possible, to an impulsive answer. This was what the Pharisees and Herodians endeavoured to do in regards to Jesus.

Could I ask you a question: Are you guilty of such behaviour? If so, why do you feel such behaviour was necessary? Before you say, of course not! Think for a moment! I remember stories when I was young, of young girls using pregnancy as a way to entrap a man. That was the method they used to fool themselves into thinking that they entrapped their husband: Little do they know the man would have married them anyway.

Let us examine the scriptures: The Pharisees sent their disciples with the Herodians, a party among the Jews, who were for full subjection to the Roman emperor. Though opposed to each other, they joined against Christ. What they said of Christ was right; whether they knew it or not. Jesus Christ was a faithful Teacher, and a bold to reprimand. Christ saw their wickedness. Whatever mask the hypocrite puts on, our Lord Jesus sees through it. Christ did not interpose as a judge in matters of this nature, for his kingdom is not of this world, but he enjoins peace-loving subjection to the powers that be. His adversaries were rebuked, and his disciples were taught that the Christian religion is no enemy to civil government. Christ is and will be, the wonder, not only of his friends but his enemies. They admire his wisdom, but will not be guided by it; They admire his wisdom his power, but will not submit to it.

They wanted to deliver him unto the power and authority of the Roman governor

Pontius Pilate, should he say anything against Caesar, which they tried to trap him into by whatever means. They wanted to set the populace against him and protect themselves from their resentment.

Their main point was the delivery of Jesus into the hands of the civil government for treason, so they could have him put to death. So here we have it they are plotting to have Jesus put to death while all the time Jesus said that is the reason he came to walk among us.

Let us look at 1 Corinthians 15:3-4: *For I delivered unto you first of all that which I also received, how that Christ died for our sins according to the scriptures; And that he was buried, and that he rose again the third day according to the scriptures:* So Jesus knew his purpose in life and it did not matter what anyone did or say the scriptures would come to pass: We also see in Luke 22:37 Jesus is speaking, and he said: *For I say unto you, that this that is written must yet be accomplished in me, And he was reckoned among the transgressors: for the things concerning me have an end.*

All this to say just like Jesus we are put here for a purpose: We are all part of a divine plan: We are not here because of accidental pregnancy, so why are we forever trying to manipulate other people into doing what we want. God plant in us a desire for something: Because we feel we must get that thing right away: We set out to connive and influence the person around us whom we see as the weakest link and could help us satisfy that desire.

Isaiah 46:10 states: *Declaring the end from the beginning, and from ancient times the things that are not yet done, saying, My counsel shall stand, and I will do all my pleasure:* So we know that God will show us the end results. The problem is getting to that end is not revealed all at once. God gives us choices as to how to arrive at the destination

You see God's power is acting in your life. There are two kinds of change: the kind that finds you and the kind you bring upon yourself. The first kind is God acting on His own to lead you in a direction; He never dictates, only suggests. The choice is always yours—to take the job offer or refuse it, to buy the house or stay where you are.

Let us get back to today's message **WHY TEMPT YE ME, YE HYPOCRITES?**

Today I am here to tell you regardless of how you scheme and try to control the person you see as the weakest link you are doing it all for naught, for the outcome will be the same. The only thing you are doing is delaying the God divine outcome and calling guilt and sickness upon yourself by harbouring negative thoughts.

Know this! The human mind cannot be the avenue for the activity of the Soul: A higher consciousness must be reached. Through this higher consciousness, through that mind which was in Christ Jesus, the Soul reveals Itself and Its activity as our individual experience. That which imparts itself to us from the inner consciousness is power, not the thoughts we think, not our statements or beliefs; but that which reveals itself from within on the inner plane is the power, with signs following.

This inner consciousness is without boundary, and, by rising to a higher level of consciousness, we become aware of that which lies far beyond our immediate knowledge. This higher consciousness is unlimited and imparts its wisdom to us infinitely and eternally. It is that insulated place within our own being, where the ceaseless activity of the outer world does not intrude.

In closing let me say this: Be aware as Jesus was when he said **WHY TEMPT YE ME, YE HYPOCRITES?** Know this! The path of each life is a choice, and some will choose to become aware after you do, and others will never be aware at all. Do not pity them, but also do not listen to their negative or doubting words. Be true to your divine truth.

PASTOR DR. GLORIA TAYLOR-BOYCE

CHAPTER 5

IS THINE EYE EVIL, BECAUSE I AM GOOD

Are you envious because of my generosity?

In Matthew 20:1-16 we have the parable of the workers in the vineyard. This Gospel serves as a corrective to false notions of entitlement and merit. The parable challenges our sense of justice. In order to grasp the full impact of the story, it is essential to understand the sequence of events in the parable.

As you listen to it, I am inviting you to place yourselves in the position of the workers who were hired at the start of the day and promised a certain wage for their day's work. Because others were hired through the course of the day and paid the amount promised, those who had worked all day long presumed they would be given more.

Matthew: 20:1-8 *For the kingdom of heaven is like unto a man that is an householder, which went out early in the morning to hire labourers into his vineyard. And when he had agreed with the labourers for a penny a day, he sent them into his vineyard. And he went out about the third hour, and saw others standing idle in the marketplace, And said unto them; Go ye also into the vineyard, and whatsoever is right I will give you. And they went their way. Again he went out about the sixth and ninth hour, and did likewise. And about the eleventh hour he went out, and found others standing idle, and saith unto them, Why stand ye here all the day idle? They say unto him, Because no man hath hired us. He saith unto them, Go ye also into the vineyard; and whatsoever is right, that shall ye receive. So when even was come, the lord of the vineyard saith unto his steward, Call the labourers, and give them their hire, beginning from the last unto the first.*

And when they had received it, they murmured against the Goodman of the house, Saying, These last have wrought but one hour, and thou hast made them equal unto us, which have borne the burden and heat of the day. But he answered one of them, and said, Friend, I do thee no wrong: didst not thou agree with me for a penny?

Take that thine is, and go thy way: I will give unto this last, even as unto thee. Is it not lawful for me to do what I will with mine own? **IS THINE EYE EVIL, BECAUSE I AM GOOD?** Are you envious because I am generous?"

There is logic in that many of us would be inclined to sympathize with these workers. It seems, in fact, to be a matter of fairness, even of justice. That is until we realize that God operates with a different logic. We want to follow a logic of strict justice, as we understand it, while God wants to act with the logic of generosity. "Why should you be envious," the landowner says to the workers, "simply because I choose to be generous?" Notice there is a sprite of envy. Know this! Envy is that fault in the human character that cannot recognize the beauty and uniqueness of the other and denies them honour. In order to approach God, who is total goodness, beauty, and generosity, this attitude must be broken from within.

Let's get back to today's scripture: The householder hires labourers for his vineyard about 6:00 a.m. for a penny, which would be considered a fair day's wage. We are already given a hint of the householder's generosity as he engages labourers at varying hours during the day.

Could it be that the householder has a compassionate concern for the unemployed and their families as opposed to actually needing them for the harvest?

The workers who were hired first appeal to common sense, equitable treatment, logic, and reason. Their complaint is not necessarily that the last hired received a payment, but that if the householder was so generous with the last, then certainly he might provide them with a "bonus" for having endured the heat of the whole day. Here we see the sense of entitlement emerging.

Some interpreters have attempted to minimize this breach of fairness by explaining that perhaps the quality of work done by the late-comers during the last hour was equivalent to the work done the entire day by the others. Certain others use the rationale that a contract is indeed a contract, and therefore the labourers hired at the beginning of the day have no reason whatsoever to argue about the wages due to them.

The fact of the matter is that from the purely human, logical point of view, they had reason to complain. However, this parable is not about ethical and fair labour management, but rather about the radical nature of God's generosity, compassion, and the in-breaking Kingdom. *"For the kingdom of heaven is like unto a man that is an householder,"*

Perhaps many of us feel strongly with the disgruntled workers of verse 12. How often have we known whimsical employers who have compensated lazy or problematic workers far too generously, rather than acknowledging the faithful and dedicated workers?

Could I ask you a question: Who is this *"householder"* that is dishing out such generosity? Tell me then why should generosity be condemned as injustice. "Let us look at what Haggai 2: 8-9 tells us: *The silver is mine, and the gold is mine, saith the Lord of hosts. The glory of this latter house shall be greater than of the former, saith the Lord of hosts: and in this place will I give peace, saith the Lord of hosts.* In essence, do not curse the messenger but recognize the source from whence it came.

We also have this word: *Except the Lord build the house, they labour in vain that built it.* Psalms: 127:1 Except the Lord builds the house, unless God is understood to be the source of our supply, there is no permanent supply. This "house" is our individual consciousness. When this consciousness is unenlightened human consciousness, it is barren; it lacks the spiritual substances from which supply flows.

Let us look at Haggai: 1:6: *Ye have sown*

much, and bring in little; ye eat, but ye have not enough; ye drink, but ye are not filled with drink; ye clothe you, but there is none warm; and he that earneth wages earneth wages to put it into a bag with holes. All this is true of you – ye the unenlightened consciousness.

As human beings, we have sown much and reaped little; we have worked hard and many times accomplished nothing; we have earned wages and often have had nothing left because all this came from a barren consciousness.

Out of the barrenness of human consciousness, regardless of what we build, our efforts are not permanent or lasting. We eat, and hunger again; we drink, and thirst again.

Let us begin to understand that the earth is

the Lord's and the fullness thereof. The *I* within us is multiplying out of the unseen resources of Spirit —not taking anything from anyone, not dividing that which is already in the world, and not drawing upon the visible resources of the earth. Now supply is multiplied from within us.

Now we are drawing forth from the invisible storehouse of our own being. Our individual consciousness is the storehouse of spiritual wealth. The moment we begin to draw from our inner storehouse, which never takes account of what is in the visible world, we cease being concerned with how much or how little we have, or whether the current economic status of the world is one of prosperity or depression. God has given to us infinite bounty, and it is unlimited in its expression as long as we recognize that the earth is the Lord's; the silver is the Lord's, and the gold is the Lord's.

In the realization that the silver is the Mine and the gold is the Mine, we draw on such infinite source that the more we use, the more remains. When we have God, we have infinite supply.

PASTOR DR. GLORIA TAYLOR-BOYCE

CHAPTER 6
EVERY SCRIPTURE WAS INSPIRED BY GOD

We are all familiar with these wonderful words from the pen of the Apostle Paul: in 2 Timothy3: 16-17 and it reads: *"Every scripture is inspired by God and useful for teaching, for reproof, for correction, and for training in righteousness, that the person dedicated to God may be capable and equipped for every good work"*. This scripture is my mantra, I live by it.

However, when it comes to today's gospel

taken from Matthew 1: 6-25 my belief in Paul's words are put to the test. Let's be honest, how many of us really find the genealogies of the Bible "useful" or "profitable"? I'll be frank with you; when it comes to genealogy, I am tempted to pass over it. And even when I do read them, I find my mind wanders, and I really don't get much out of it until this week as I work on today's homily.

We know that there are two genealogies of our Lord in the Gospels. The first we immediately encounter in Matthew 1; the second is found later on in Luke 3:23-38. Matthew's genealogy has three divisions. It begins with Abraham and goes forward, ending with the Lord Jesus Christ. Luke's genealogy begins with Jesus, and then going backward takes us to Adam, the **"son of God."**

Now Matthew believes a genealogy makes a good introduction hence it is in the first chapter of the New Testament. I also think that it speaks to our ancestry and our heritage and it is on that basis that I want to talk about "Ye Are the Temple"!

Before I get into *"Ye Are the Temple"* as outlined in 1 Corinthians 16:19 I just wanted you to know that in real life, most of us do believe that genealogies are profitable. Think about this when you are paying a good price to purchase anything. Do you not automatically become interested in where that item came from? If it is a dog, you will be interested in the animal's pedigree (or genealogy).

Look at this! In today's society with its many mix races, some people have gone to considerable effort to trace their own genealogy because they want to know who their ancestors were. There are many reasons for people to be interested in genealogies. Nonetheless, it is at this point I am going to shift gears so we can understand our own true genealogy: 1 Corinthians 16:19 states *Know ye not that ye are the temple of God*....That your body is the temple...of the living God.

MATTHEW 1:6-25

Your body is the temple of the living God, a temple not made with hands, not mortally conceived, but eternal in the heavens, that is, eternal in time and space; eternal in life; eternal in spirit, in soul, and in substance, God made all that was made, and all that God made as made of God, partaking of the very nature of God which is eternality, immortality, and perfection. God made the body in His own image and likeness.

Now I want you all to hear me! God is life. An activity of God, operating in a seed, brings forth a child with all the potentialities of adulthood embodied in one tiny form– not merely a piece of matter, but intelligence and a soul accompanying that body. Are you hearing me, somebody? The Spirit of God does this, but man in his vanity has arrogated to himself the role of a creator. Men and women have assumed that because they were fathers and mothers, they were originators, instead of knowing that they are the instruments through which God acts to express Himself–not to perpetuate you or me, or my children or your children. God operates as love in our consciousness to produce His own image and likeness.

This expression of God; we have called your child and mine, forgetting, that this is God's child, and not a personal creation and a personal possession. We pray to God to maintain and sustain our children, but they are not our children; they are God's children. It is not necessary to pray that God maintains and sustains His own children. It is God's prerogative to create, maintain, and sustain His own image and likeness.

God is the creator of all that is. God then, is the creator of man's body: Know ye not that your body is the temple of the living God. We call this body your body and my body, but it is not ours. It is God's body, formed by Him for His pleasure, made is His image and likeness, governed by His law, and created to show forth His glory.

Okay let us put it in real terms: On our Christmas trees, there are lights of all colours, red, blue and purple. Electricity transmits its lights through these multi-coloured bulbs of all shapes and sizes. The bulbs in and of themselves, are not the sources of the light; they are merely the instruments through which the light shines.

So, it is that when we see humans, we mistake their visible form for the life which lives and is the substance of that form. God is the life and the substance of all form, the creative principle of all that is. God is the activity governing the functions and organs of the body. It is God that is breathing in all men and women. God is the wisdom, the integrity, and the purity of the Soul of man. God is the strength of man.

Let us not be deceived by appearances, not even by good appearances. Let us not call one person strong and another one beautiful. We must look behind the appearance of the invisible Life which makes all this beauty of form possible. Then we can enjoy every aspect of creation, every appearance, whether it is the human body, an animal species, or a plant. These are forms of life, but if we do not understand that Life which vitalizes these forms, they may appear as either good or bad, young or old, sick or well rich or poor.

What I am saying is this! A limited human sense of life relies on shifting values, and invests the forms life assumes, <u>with power for good or evil</u>; a spiritual sense of life, however, enjoys the form while recognizing the Infinite Invisible as the essence of that form. Look at this! If we take our eyes away from the form long enough to look behind it into the Invisible and see God as the principle of all life, we shall understand the difference between <u>material living and spiritual living</u>. The truth entertained in our consciousness is the law of life, of harmony, and of resurrection unto our body.

God made this form, my infinite divine form, to show forth my true identity. My body is a manifestation, the image of the I that I am. My body is an expression of life showing forth all that I am, because my body is the "I" that I am formed, and formed spiritually, eternally, and immortally. I am a true identity–eternal identity–and my body is the temple, the instrument of my activity and of my living.

As against this spiritual truth, there is that form which I see in a mirror; there are the expressions of nature, such as trees, flowers, vegetables, and fruits. These are not spiritual being or body: these are the concepts that are entertained humanly of being and body.

If I look in a mirror, I may see myself as young or old, sick or well, stout or thin, but I am not seeing myself at all. I am seeing my body. That is my body, but "I" am invisible. Even this body which I see with my eyes is but a limited, finite concept of the body. That is the reason the body appears to keep changing. In reality, the body never changes; only the concept which I entertain about body changes.

Who am I? What am I? Where am I? Let us look down at our feet and ask ourselves Is this I? Are these feet I or are they mine? Am I in the feet or do I possess these feet? Let us travel on up to the knee. Am I in the legs or are these legs **mine**? If they are injured, am I hurt; or is it my legs that are injured?

Is there not an I, an identity which is not the legs? Let us go up to the waist, to the chest, the neck, and finally the head. Am I in any of these or are these parts of the body **mine?** Is there not an I separate and apart from the body, an I which possess the body? The body is an instrument for the activity, my movement, as much mine as is my automobile. **Are you hearing me somebody?** Am I in the ears, eyes, mouth, tongue, throat, or are they **mine**? Is it not a temple, an instrument given too me for my use?

Look at my hands. Can they of themselves give or withhold, or must I give or withhold using the hands as an instrument in either case? Can my hands be generous or miserly? Have my hands the power to give or the power to withhold; or does that power resides in me? Is there not something called "I" that gives through these hands? Is there not something called "I" which functions through this body? Is there not something called "I" which walks the street through these legs or by means of these legs? Is there not something called "I" which functions through the instrumentality of this body?

As I get ready to close, **know this**! My being is not dependent upon body. **My body** is dependent upon my being. The "I" that I am governs my body. My body has no will of its own, no intelligence of its own, no action of its own. My body responds to me. I govern it. My body is the image and likeness of me. My body is the manifestation of me, the **I** that **I AM**. There is a Spirit in me: the breath of the Almighty giveth me life.

The activity of God in me governs my bodily

functions, organs, and muscles. An invisible Spirit acts upon every organ and function of my body to maintain it and sustain it unto eternity. Nothing from without, to defile or make a lie, can enter this temple of the living God. Whatever is of God, God will maintain and sustain. Whatever is the truth about my body will live forever because my body is the temple of the living God.

PASTOR DR. GLORIA TAYLOR-BOYCE

CHAPTER 7

THE GREAT AWAKENING

And there was a cloud that overshadowed them: and a voice came out of the cloud, saying, This is my beloved Son: hear him. And suddenly, when they had looked round about, they saw no man any more, save Jesus only with themselves.

Today I want to talk about the great awakening for many of us are sleepwalking: Romans 13:11 states: *And that, knowing the time, that now it is high time to awake out of sleep: for now is our salvation nearer than when we believed.*

Now it is high time to awake out of sleep. The belief in a life apart from God is a dream from which we must awake, if we are to taste the waters of Reality, which flow from the Sources of life. You can never be happy without inner peace, and things do not give you peace A connection to the inner Christ gives you peace.

As one awakes from a nightmare, so we must mentality awake from the dream of a living death to a realization of eternal life. We cast off the works of darkness when we realize that evil is not an entity, a body, an individual, but a fraud. The armour of light is the Truth, the very knowledge of which makes us free.

This awakening is a process of evolution, a little here and a little there, until the whole eye is opened, and we see that life is neither separate from God nor different from Good. Life is God, and Good is the only power there is or can be.

To awaken oneself is to be healed, made prosperous, happy and satisfied; to be made whole, to be complete as we were intended to be. God is a God of the living and not of the dead. He sees and knows only perfection, completion, happiness and satisfaction. When we shall think of ourselves as *God* knows us, then complete salvation will come to us.

11Corinthians 3:17 tells us: Now the Lord is that Spirit: and where the Spirit of the Lord is, there is liberty.

The law of God is one of liberty and not of bondage. Know this! Freedom and liberty are also everywhere if we could but see them. Freedom, like Truth, is self-existent and self-propelling. The Spirit, Truth, and Freedom are co-existent with one another.

Whenever we are conscious of God, or pure Spirit, we are made free. This is proven in mental and spiritual healing. When we are conscious of *perfect life,* the body is healed. We must become unconscious of the imperfect and conscious of the perfect alone. Since our ideas of perfection are limited to our present understanding, we do not yet manifest perfection. With a greater unfoldment of Reality through our consciousness, we shall evolve a more perfect body.

In the demonstration of abundance, we seek to realize the liberty of the Sons of God – the freedom whereby God proves His absoluteness. This is done, not by meditation upon limitation, but by contemplating plenty, abundance, success, prosperity and happiness. Remember we are always falling forward; not backward.

Also, it is unscientific to dwell upon lack, for it will create that undesired condition. It is scientific to meditate on plenty, to bring the mind to a point of conceiving an eternal flow of life, truth, and energy through us... **and through everything that we do, say or think.**

The question is; how do we Demonstrate Liberty?

To demonstrate liberty, we must drop all negative thoughts from the mind. Do not dwell upon adversity but think plenty into everything, **for there is power in the word**. Meditate on the things you are doing as being already done – complete and perfect.

Try to sense the Infinite Life around and within you. This life is already fully expressed and complete. This life is your life ***now,*** and the life of all that you do, say or think. Meditate upon this Life until your whole being flows into it and becomes one with it.

Now you are ready to prove your principle by allowing this Life to flow through the thing that you are working on or for. Do not will or try to compel things to happen. Things happen by an immutable law; an unchallengeable law; and you do not need to energize the Essence of Being; It is already big with power. All you need do is to realize this fact, and then let it be done unto you, or unto that for which you are working. L-E-T is a big word and an important one. By taking thought, you do not add one cubit to Reality, but you do allow (let) Reality to manifest in the things you are doing.

As the power of your meditation is centered on what you are doing, life flows through that thing, living it with real power and action, which ends in the desired results. The Spirit of God is loosed in your work. Where this Spirit is, there is liberty. 11 CORINTHIANS talks to us about mental expression:

Mental expansion (11 Corinthians 3:18)

But we all, with open face beholding as in a glass the glory of the Lord, are changed into the same image from glory to glory even as by the Spirit of the Lord.

As our thought is opened and we behold the image of eternity within ourselves, we are changed by this image into a newness of Life. This is accomplished by the Spirit of God.

The subjective state of thoughts is the creative medium within us, which fact

has proven beyond any question of doubt. It is said that we are inlets and might become outlets to the Divine Nature. *We are already inlets*, but we must *consciously become outlets*. I once heard it said this way; that the upper part of the soul is merged with God and the lower part with time and conditions. Jesus tells us to seek the Kingdom of God first, and all else will be added unto us.

Now the image of God is imprinted upon each one of us, and all reflect the Divine Glory to some degree. Indeed, we are part of the greater glory, we then reflect that glory. When our thoughts are turned from limitation to the greater glory, we then reflect that glory.

When the subjective state of receives its images from Reality reflects this Reality into all Gradually, as the process takes place, the outer man becomes changed, and as his concepts become enlarged, so his conditions and physique take on a newness of life.

And this change in the outer is brought about by the Spirit of God. The Spirit of God – being the One and Only Presence in the Universe – brings about events and re-molds conditions after its own likeness. Now let us look at the ascending scale of life 11 Corinthians 3:7-12 from the message bible reads as such:

The Ascending Scale Of Life 11 Corinthians 3:7-12

The Government of Death, its constitution chiseled on stone tablets, had a dazzling opening. Moses' face as he delivered the tablets was so bright that day (even though it would fade soon enough) that the people of Israel could no more look right at him than stare into the sun. How much more dazzling, then, is the Government of Living Spirit? If the Government of Condemnation was impressive, how about this Government of Affirmation? Bright as that old government was, it would look downright dull alongside this new one. If that makeshift arrangement impressed us, how much more this brightly shining government installed for eternity? With that kind of hope to excite us, nothing holds us back.

In closing, I want to talk about the Ascending Scale for we changed from glory to glory. This implies that the divine scale is ever ascending. There is no end to the Divine Nature and therefore no end to the possibility of our expressing It. BUT WE MUST BEHOLD IT, we must look steadfastly into this Reality if we are to image It in our minds.

Right here is no hopeless outlook, no limited concept! All that God has, or IS, belongs to us and is ours to make use of. We are not to separate Life from living but unite the two into a perfect One.

The world is saturated with Divinity, deep in Reality, and filled with possibility. We must take this divine possibility and mold it into a present activity in everyday experience. This is the way to freedom, the pathway to peace and happiness. Now we all receive divine ideas 11 CORINTHIANS 4:8-9 states: *We are troubled on every side, yet not distressed; we are perplexed, but not in despair; Persecuted, but not forsaken; cast down, but not destroyed; The Divine Ideas 11 Corinthians 4: 8, 9*

Even in our troubles we are not cast down, and through we appear to be deserted, we are not destroyed. All our experiences are working to the end that we learn the lesson of life and return to the Father's House as freed souls.

We should not despise apparent failures– the temporary chagrins of life – for they are helpful, leading the soul to the inner Christ, the Way, the Truth, and the Life. When the experience is complete, the lesson will be learnt, and we shall enter the – paradise of contentment.

We do not look at the things which are seen as being eternal. Behind the visible and changeable is the changeless reality, the Eternal One, working in time and space for the expression of Itself. The Divine Ideas stand back of all human thought, seeking admittance through the doorway of the mind.

If we look at love long enough, we shall become lovely, for this is the way of love. God is Love. If we gaze longingly at joy, it will make its home with us, and we shall enter its portals and be happy. If we seek the Divine in men, we shall find it, and be entertaining angels unawares.

God ideas and attributes are eternal and cannot change. In change is the Changeless. In time, is the Eternal and Timeless. In things, the Creator manifests his power and glory forevermore.

PASTOR DR. GLORIA TAYLOR-BOYCE

CHAPTER 8
JESUS SAID TO THEM, COME WITH ME!

Teaching and Healing: Matthew 4:12-23

When Jesus got word that John had been arrested, he returned to Galilee. He moved from his hometown, Nazareth, to the lakeside village Capernaum, nestled at the base of the Zebulun and Naphtali hills. This move completed Isaiah's sermon: about *people sitting out their lives in the dark saw a huge light; Sitting in that dark, dark country of death, they watched the sun come up.*

This Isaiah-prophesied sermon came to life in Galilee the moment Jesus started preaching. He picked up where John left off: "Change your life. God's kingdom is here." Walking along the beach of Lake Galilee, Jesus saw two brothers: Simon (later called Peter) and Andrew. They were fishing, throwing their nets into the lake. It was their regular work. Jesus said to them, **"Come with me.** I'll make a new kind of fisherman out of you. I'll show you how to catch men and women instead of perch and bass."

They didn't ask questions, but simply dropped their nets and followed. A short distance down the beach they came upon another pair of brothers, James and

John, Zebedee's sons. These two were sitting in a boat with their father, Zebedee, mending their fishnets. Jesus made the same offer to them, and they were just as quick to follow, abandoning boat and father." In spiritual literature and in the Scriptures, there are many references which might indicate to you that you must change your way of life or you must do something in order to earn the grace of God. I want you to remember what I am saying to you today! The responsibility is not on your shoulders, nor is it on any other person's shoulders. Therefore, I ask you to refrain from all indulgence in criticism or judgment of anyone in the world, and more particularly judgment, criticism, condemnation, and belittling of yourself and your own understanding because the responsibility to improve yourself is not on your shoulders' it is on the shoulders of the Christ.

I am asking you today to rest more in the realization of the Christ as that which is leading, guiding, and directing you. Never believe that the saints and seers of the world came about it, by some great act of their own will, because it is not true.

I can tell you that I did not give up my personal professional by my own will and grace, but rather that the grace of God pulled me out of the business world and made me **FELLOW HIM**.

The Master walked the hillsides and as he chose each disciple, his promise was, "Follow me, and I will make you fishers of men" and He is still walking today and saying Follow-Me and I will make you fishers of men. Perhaps you think that they were men of high understanding because they obeyed. No, they had no power not to obey. They had no more power to resist the Master than you and I have right now. When the Master says, fellow me, and I will make you fishers of men **YOU WILL OBEY.**

Could I tell you that you have already obeyed in the sacrifice of time, money, effort, study, and the service you are all making to your ministry here at Saint Zoe Parish Church? You have already shown that you have no capacity to resist the activity of the Christ in your consciousness, even if you had the will or the desire, which of course, you do not have. But if you had, and if you lacked the understanding, the wisdom, courage, or the determination, it still would make no difference because there is that in you which is greater than your human sense of rebellion or your desire for ease in the matter.

Yes, the human being has a normal, natural desire to be at ease, but few human beings spend their time, effort, and money to learn more about God as you have already done. Oh no! The human being has weddings to attend and funerals, and people to help out of the ditch. The human being has so many things to occupy him – tickets for theatres, meetings to attend, sports events that he does not respond to the activity of the Christ. But once the finger has touched a person, and he is called, rest assured that he will follow. After the Master called them out did the disciples suffered no! They went on and they survived. He took some to the mountaintop! He Took Them! Did they go by themselves? No! Nor have you, nor have I.

This is a life by grace. Everything that transpires in your life today and everything that transpires from now unto eternity is and will be, an act of grace.

Oh, I know there are a few of you, and maybe I am one of those few, who will resist that call for a little while. Here and there you will turn aside to indulge in some personal sense, some personal will, some personal ambition, but you will be forced back because it is not given to you to resist the Christ. It is not given to you to refuse the call when it comes. True you may be guilty of betrayal: you may be guilty of falling asleep in your Garden of Gethsemane. What difference does it make? Do not be disturbed by it; do not be alarmed by it. Do not condemn yourself for your shortcomings. Just realize that it is part of the illusion that may be to be expected, but because of divine grace, ultimate salvation is even more predictable.

I can tell you that every one of you here today has answered the call. Whatever you are doing today you are guiding from within: Remember God is the one calling us out! If you were to pause for a moment, close your eyes, and look inside, you would realize that; you have never had the peace that you have right now. You have never felt the love of God so strong upon you. And you will see that all your concerns have nothing to do with you, but are all for someone else. Why is that you may ask? You are under God's grace!

As a result, today I am asking you for Patience! Patience! You have an eternity in which to work out your salvation. Patience! Be patient with one another and be patient with yourself. Forgive yourself, and as often as you fall down, pick yourself up again. You have no choice! Inevitably, the voice will sound in your ear. Come Fellow me and I will make you fishers of men.

PASTOR DR. GLORIA TAYLOR-BOYCE

CHAPTER 9

ABUNDANCE IS YOUR INHERITANCE

"...I am come that they might have life, and that they might have it more abundantly." *(John 10:10)*

Infinite Supply... It's Yours!

Abundance is yours. You cannot be deprived of God's supply. No one can deprive you of what God has ordained for you. If you observe the lavish wastefulness of nature, you can discern that the Father intended for his children to be abundantly supplied, to lack for nothing, to want for nothing.

"Consider the lilies of the field, how they grow; they toil not, neither do they spin: And yet I say unto you, that even Solomon in all his glory was not arrayed like one of these." (Matthew 6:28-29)

All blessings come from God. However, we cannot manipulate God, force Him or box Him in to receive His blessings. Just because of whom you are and who the Father created you to be, you have the power to command happiness in your life. When you know the truth of your being, you will no longer hinder or retard the good of God from coming to you.

You are a child of the Spirit, and every attribute of God and good is your inheritance. You must accept and expect the fact that only you can make life happy and worthwhile for you. Only the lack of faith can keep your good from reaching you. You must hold on to that truth.

We cannot control the blessings of God. God will manifest His blessings according to our faith in Him. However, we are to prepare a place for the blessings and make sure that we are walking in divine order. That is it. That is all we have to do. It is not by the sweat of your brow, but it is by the way that you think. Your thought process can either hinder you or move you forward.

Revelation 3:20 says, *"Behold, I stand at the door, and knock: if any man hear my voice, and open the door, I will come in to him, and will sup with him, and he with me."*

Who is the "I" that stands at the door and at what door is the "I" standing? Is the "I" yourself or the God that dwells within you? The "I" is God. The "door" is your consciousness. God-in-you stands at the door of your consciousness and knocks! You must open your mind (your consciousness) and admit Him. The "I" is the bread of life." (John 6:35) The "I" is the way, the truth and the life. (John 14:16) The "I" is the resurrection and the life. (John 11:25) It is that "I" who comes that you might have life and have that life more abundantly. (John 10:10) That "I" is standing at the door of your consciousness and knocking!

When you admit that "I" is your consciousness, you admit life eternal, the bread of life, the water of life, the wine of life. You admit into your consciousness the power of the resurrection. There are often times when people hear the word "resurrection" they only refer to the resurrection of Jesus Christ. However, the Bible says that the Christ lives in us. (Romans 8:9) The Father knew you before you entered your mother's womb. When I refer to the "resurrection", I am referring to the resurrection of your body, the resurrection of your home, the resurrection of your marriage, the resurrection of your good fortune, the resurrection of your business, the resurrection of your dreams.

Only when you admit the "I" into your consciousness, do you admit into yourself the sacredness of life. When you acknowledge that the "I" in the midst of you is mighty, you are not speaking of a human being. You are speaking of the great "I AM," God himself.

Close your eyes for a minute and within yourself, silently, sacredly and gently affirm, "I." Say it until you can feel the power thereof. That "I" that is in the midst of you is mighty. That "I" that is in the midst of you is greater than any problem in the outside world. That "I" that is in the midst of you has come that you might have life and has it more abundantly. That "I" that has been with you since before Abraham was, awaiting your recognition and your acknowledgment.

"Know ye not that you are the temple of God?" (1 Corinthians 6:15) Do you not know that the name of God is I or I Am and that you are the temple of God? Only when you have admitted "I" into your consciousness, and held it there secretly, sacredly, gently and peacefully, so that at any moment you can close your eyes and

just remember it, will you experience the true power of God in your life. And the infinite blessings and abundance that are rightfully yours and come as a result of your faith. You must affirm, *"The 'I' in the midst of me is eternal. The 'I' that is within me is mighty."*

The Christ Within

"I am crucified with Christ: nevertheless I live; yet not I, but Christ liveth in me: and the life which I now live in the flesh I live by the faith of the Son of God, who loved me, and gave himself for me." (Galatians 2:20)

In Galatians 2:20, when Paul speaks of the Christ that dwells in him, he is referring to the "I Am," the very "I" that you are, the "I" that is in the midst of you. The way to avoid suffering from a dose of egotism, and to differentiate between the egotistical "I", (the "I" that believes it has power, and sufficient wisdom to rule the world, or even sufficient wisdom to run its own life), and the "I" in the midst of everyone (the gentle, sacred, and powerful "I") is to recognize that you cannot use or influence God. By yielding to the divine "I" God can use you.

You cannot influence God. It is only when you yield to the divine "I" within you, that God will influence you, guide you, direct you, feed you, clothe you and provide shelter for you. Your heavenly Father, the "I" that you are, knows that you have need of all of these things. It is the Father's good pleasure to give you the kingdom. (Luke 12:32) If the ego strikes at you so that even for a moment you believe God is subject to your way, remember quickly it is not your will that will be done, but God's will. God's will can be done only to the degree of your yielding to the "I" within you.

You are walking in the Spirit of God. You have that Spirit of God within you. You know that there is a Supreme Being. There is a power greater than yourself. You are Spirit.

"...the LORD God made the earth and the heavens, and every plant of the field before it was in the earth, and every herb of the field before it grew..." (Genesis 2:4-5)

The one question that many people in the world of thought ponder is whether a person has the capacity, equipment, and power to control his life, whether he can be what he wants to be or whether he is a drop in the great ocean of life. Millions are affected by unemployment, poverty, and want. Can they help it? Where there are broken homes broken and family problems, can such breach be repaired? Millions complain of sickness and disorder in countless forms. All this gives rise to the belief that we are victims of circumstances over which we have no control. However, such belief makes us fatalists instead of masters of our destiny.

Do not buy into that belief system. A fatalist's belief is contagious. When people submit to the influence and belief of a fatalist, believing that the circumstances around them are stronger than the power within them, they are defeated before they even start. If you think that the outside conditions are greater than what is in you, you are dead before you even start living.

In the history of Man, there is overwhelming evidence of Man overcoming circumstances and meeting challenges in life. Evolution and anthropology support the truth that Man is responsible for his condition. He has the power to control his circumstances. By using this power, he creates other circumstances more necessary in his upward climb. However, there are those who are not sure that we create our circumstances and are prone to think that their problems and challenges are hereditary or a result of karma, the environment or numerous other external factors.

They blame the external factors for their failures in life. They believe in the natural limitation of life. They live in the conviction that they are unsure where they are and what they will become. This type of belief system must be changed. The belief that you are a victim of your environment, your colour, your race or where you were born, must be eradicated if you want to break the cycle of limitation and lack in your life and move forward.

The scientists searching the mysteries of life reveal to us a wonderful world of power, possibilities, and promise. They tell us that the mind is the creative cause of all results in our lives, that personal conditions are the result of our actions, and that our actions are the direct result of our ideas.

You never make a move of any kind until you first form some image, plan, or idea in mind. These images, plans, and ideas are powerful and potent. They are the cause (good, bad or indifferent) of the subsequent effects, which in turn correspond to their nature. The scientists believe that these ideas generate tremendous energy. Hence, when we learn to employ our mind constructively, we use these hidden powers, forces and faculties correctly. According to the scientists, this is the key to successful living.

However, in the spiritual realm, there is a marvellous inner world that exists within Man. The revelation of such a world enables him to do, to attain and to achieve anything he desires within the bounds or limits of nature. If everyone has the power and privilege to determine his/her fortune, how do we identify this inner power? If all conditions are the result of our actions, and our actions are the outcome of the fruit of our ideas, then our ideas must determine the conditions of our daily life.

The Creative Power of the Mind

"In the beginning God created the heaven and the earth. And the earth was without

form, and void; and darkness was upon the face of the deep. And the Spirit of God moved upon the face of the waters." (Genesis 1:1-2)

An idea is a thought or a group of thoughts, an image or a picture in mind. There is an idea or a mental picture behind every well-known achiever or invention. The mind has creative power. From the beginning of time, this creative power was implemented by the Great Architect, God himself, as outlined in the first book of the Bible. God had a pattern and a plan for growth. He had an idea that grew. There was a mental picture established within the Creator's mind before it became a reality.

The Lord God made the earth and the heavens and every plant in the field before it was in the earth and every herb of the field before it grew. Everything must be created in Spirit. That is the truth of who you are. You have to go to the Source. Stop fighting over the spoils in life; those are effects. Go to the Source for everything that you need. Go to the Source to implement your creative power. You have the Infinite Source, the Source that never dries up living on the inside of you. Go to the Source for everything. You have to learn to go within yourself to create that which you need in your natural experience.

Every architect follows a plan, whether he is building a house, a bridge, an institution or his own life. Every man is his own designer and builder. Like the Creator, he makes his creations within, before they materialize on the outside. All fears of sickness, poverty, old age, and depression are mental pictures and ideas long before they become some painful reality. No one wants to inflict pain and suffering on themselves willingly. However, when you allow negative thoughts to overshadow the creative power of your mind, then you subject yourself to pain.

"For as he thinketh in his heart, so is he..." (Proverbs 23:7)

Negative self-talk, negative self-images and negative feelings about yourself can lead to self-destruction. To combat the negative self-talk, negative self-images, and negative feelings about oneself, it is paramount to begin to build, what Neuro-Linguistic Programming (NLP) calls, a "rapport" with yourself. Rapport means to enter into congruency with someone or something, a close, harmonious relationship. When you say you are in rapport with something or someone, it means that you are congruent with them.

Humans experience life through the five senses: sight, hearing, touch, smell, and taste. According to the teachings in NLP, negative thoughts attack our three main sensory receivers: auditory, visual and kinesthetic. Negative self-talk relates to auditory; negative self-images relate to visual, and feelings of negativity relate to kinesthetic. Negative thoughts form patterns and those patterns form your belief system.

If you are not experiencing the abundant life that God has commissioned for you, you must change your belief system. You have to guard the gate of your mind more closely. Nobody is exempt from negative thinking, negative self-talk, negative self-image and negative feelings about oneself. However, if you want to experience all that God has for you, you have to implement the techniques that will arrest these negative thoughts early so that they do not take root in your conscious mind and express themselves in your outside world as reality.

Every idea or mental picture must produce after its kind, whether good, bad or indifferent. It is the law of cause and effect. The law of cause and effect does not question or challenge a person's mental pictures, images and thoughts. It takes what is planted for it to be materialized into a visual form.

Some men can visualize great engineering achievements. Yet, many are not aware that by using the same technique of visualization they can overcome sickness and disease in their bodies. The same visualization techniques used to picture a house or create a portrait are the same techniques used to visualize yourself perfect and whole. It's the same principle.

A picture of a homely person never develops into a picture of a beautiful pageant winner, nor does the short person look tall in a photograph. A picture will only mirror the image projected.

A story was told of a woman who once lived in a beautiful home, in an exclusive suburban area. She was happy. She had every comfort imaginable. The home was large; it had a fence, a beautiful lake, a nice flower gardens. She had servants to help her maintain the property. She was living the life of which many people could only dream. Yet, she began to say within herself, *"I don't need this big house. All I want is a little room for myself. That's all I need. This house is too large. All I want is a little room, a little place that I could just keep clean."*

A few years later, her husband died and left her the estate. She sold the house. Unfortunately, as a result of the downward spiral in the economy, her other holdings and investments diminished in value to nothing. Unable to rebound financially, she was forced to rent a small room in someone else's home. That which she visualized in her mind over time became her reality

As we assimilate the negative ideas and mental pictures, we consciously and sometimes unconsciously exercise our power to produce them. This creative process continues working night and day until the idea is completed. We cannot picture thoughts of poverty, failure, disease and doubt and expect to experience wealth, success, health and courage. Your outward picture will always represent your inward thoughts. *"As a man thinketh in his heart, so is he."* (Proverbs 23:7)

Building Rapport Within

In order to move forward in life and dismantle the negative thoughts in your mind, you must develop a rapport with yourself. You must be congruent with your thoughts. If you are not able to develop congruency with your thoughts, you will block your blessings.

To maximize effective communication with others, it is important to have a good relationship with yourself. In other words, you should have a rapport with yourself. Our natural state is to be in rapport with ourselves. However, as we grow older, we lose this connection. We become more self-conscious, which results in self-assessment.

Negative self-assessment, whether it is negative self-talk, negative self-imaging or negative feelings of oneself, whether visual, auditory or kinesthetic is detrimental to experiencing and exercising personal power. If you give credence to negative self-talk, negative self-imaging, or negative feelings of oneself, it is detrimental to your personal power. You hinder your God-self. You self-impose limitations that cause you to be stagnant. You interrupt your natural state, and in doing so you block rapport with yourself.

Negative self-talk is one of the most insidious ways we block rapport and sabotage ourselves. It results in personal misery. When you hear yourself entering into negative self-talk, you should immediately stop, pull yourself out of its negative spiral and begin to reframe your thoughts. One simple strategy for doing this is to say "stop" as soon as you hear it. This will interrupt the negative self-talk and give you an opportunity to face your negative thoughts and deal with them accordingly. You can give yourself a pep talk. Don't have a pity party. Just stop the negative self-talk in its tracks.

Negative self-imaging is another detriment to our personal power. There are times when we deplete our personal power by our negative self-imaging. We see in our mind's eye previews of coming attractions, and the movies are often not pleasant ones. How do we turn off these previews? How do we turn on the movies that will give us the pleasant realities?

There is a powerful technique used to reclaim the screening room of your mind. It is called the "swish pattern." You can reclaim the screening room in your mind. The thoughts in your head are like a movie. They are like a preview of a movie playing over and over and over. If you don't like the movie that is playing in your mind, you can change it. The swish pattern can be likened to the picture in the future.

You may be familiar with the picture-in-a-picture feature found in many televisions. This feature enables you to have two channels on the screen at the same time, a large, full-screen picture and a smaller picture in the corner of the bigger picture. If something of a greater interest appears on the smaller screen, you can then switch the image to the larger screen, causing what was on the larger screen to now appear in the smaller window.

You can implement this same technique when changing negative self-images that form in your mind. You can use the "swish pattern" to change any negative image that comes to your mind. First, create a picture of the desired state and then insert that desired state in the smaller window of your mental screen. In other words, the state that you desire goes into the small screen. This can be either a still image or a series of moving pictures. The negative image that is dominating your mind is not the one you want. Create a desire that you want. After you put the desired state on the smaller screen, swish (or switch) it so that the desired state is projected on the bigger screen of your mind.

As you swish the images so that the larger, undesired state becomes the smaller, desired state only the desired state remains. Your ultimate objective is to have the positive image become most dominant in your mind. Assume the power to choose which channel you want to watch in your mind, rather than allowing unwanted channels to beam in some insidious internal deliberating process. You are in control of the pictures in your mind, and it is, therefore, your choice which images are dominant. You have a choice. You do not have to suffer.

"Casting down imaginations, and every high thing that exalteth itself against the knowledge of God, and bringing into captivity every thought to the obedience of Christ." (2 Corinthians 10:5)

Affirmation:

I want you to repeat the following affirmation that will keep the negative self-talk, negative self-images and negative feelings at bay and allow you to manifest the blessings of God in your life. I want you in a quiet, relaxed state. I want you to become one with the Father within you. Put your feet flat on the ground. Take a deep breath in and out and repeat...

Father, within me is the infinite, the limitless spiritual universe. Let it flow. Let it be the avenue of healing the multitudes, feeding the multitudes, of understanding, helping, companioning and aiding them. Let all of this flow as a service unto thee, in Jesus' Mighty Name.

PASTOR DR. GLORIA TAYLOR-BOYCE

CHAPTER 10

CLAIM YOUR TRUTH

"And ye shall know the truth, and the truth shall make you free." *(John 8:32)*

Be Not Afraid...Success is Your Birthright!

"Fear thou not; for I am with thee: be not dismayed; for I am thy God: I will strengthen thee; yea, I will help thee; yea, I will uphold thee with the right hand of my righteousness." (Isaiah 41:10)

Frequently, in scripture when the angel of the Lord appeared, the first thing the angel would say is, *"Be not afraid."* You cannot be afraid to claim your truth. What is your truth?

Did you know that success is your birthright? If a man constantly has thoughts of sickness, poverty, and misfortune, eventually he will encounter them in his life and claim them as his own. He will fail to acknowledge his close relationships with God. He will even deny his own children and declare they were sent to him by an evil fate. Yet, he refuses to accept that abundance and prosperity is his birthright. No man has a right (unless he cannot help himself) to remain where he is constantly subjected to cramped ambition, blighted influence and great temptations of poverty.

No man has a right to stay in that kind of an

environment. His self-respect demands that he should get out of such an environment. It is his duty to put himself in a position of dignity and independence, where he will not be subjected, at any moment, to be a burden on his friends, in case of sickness or another emergency, or where those depending on him may suffer.

The wealthy person will tell you that his greatest satisfaction and happiest days were when he was emerging from scarcity into proficiency, when he first felt the force from the swelling of his small saving into the flow of fortune and knew that lack would no longer control his life. What a great feeling. It was then he began to see ahead of his leisure and self-development or perhaps fine homes, travel and the relief that his loved ones would be lifted from the clutches of lack.

Comforts take the place of stern necessity and blundering drudgery. He realizes that he has the power to lift himself above his current state, that henceforth, he would be of consequence in the world, that he will have the luxuries and comforts of life (pictures, music, books), and that his children, unlike himself, will not have to struggle to receive a good education. He senses the invigorating power in being able to give them and others a start in the world and the satisfaction of watching the little circle around him expand into a larger sphere, broadening into a wider horizon.

Lack and want do not fit Man's divine DNA.

There is overwhelming evidence in scripture that we were made for grand and inspiring things, for plenty and not for deficiency.

The problem is many people do not have enough faith to receive the good that God pre-ordained for them from the beginning. Many dare not break away from their soul's desire to follow the leading of their divine hunger and ask without stint for the abundance that is their birthright. They ask for small things and expect small things, pinching their desires and limiting their supply, daring not to ask the fullness of their soul's desire.

They refuse to open their minds sufficiently to allow the great inflow of good things into their lives. Their mentality is controlled with self-expression and subdued to the point that they think thoughts of meanness and inadequacy. Many struggle to fling out their soul's desire with the abundant faith that trusts implicitly and receives accordingly.

The power that made and sustains us gives to everyone and everything liberally and abundantly, not stingily. There is no restriction, no limitation, and no loss to anyone as a result of God's abundant giving. The rose does not ask the sun for only a small fraction of its light and heat. It is the sun's nature to give its energy to everything that will absorb it. The candle loses none of its light by lighting another candle. Likewise, the Creator does not lack as a result of granting our requests. He does not have less because we ask for much. It is God's nature to give to his children and to flood us with our heart's desires.

By being friendly and giving abundantly of our love, we do not lose but increase our capacity for friendship. One of the greatest secrets of life is to learn how to transfer the full current of divine force to ourselves and use this force effectively. If Man can discover and apply this law of divine transfer to his life, he will multiply his efficiency a million-fold. He will be a co-operator, a co-creator with the divine on a scale of which he has never before dreamed.

When we recognize that everything comes from the Infinite Supply (God) and flows through us freely, when we get in perfect tune with the Infinite, when the brut has been educated out of us and droves of dishonesty, selfishness and impurity burned out of us, we will see God without the scales that blind us to our good. We shall see God. We shall see our good. We shall know our good. Only the pure in heart can see God. (Matthew 5:8)

Divorcing Lack and Limitation

If you allow unfairness and the desire to

take advantage of your brothers and sisters to be removed from your life, you will become so close to God that all of the good in the universe will flow spontaneously to you. However, many people restrict the inflow of good into their lives by engaging in wrongful acts and thinking wrong thoughts.

Every vicious deed is a veil, a film over our eyes so that we cannot see God and, as a result, we are blinded from our good. Every wrong step separates us from Him. When you learn the art of seeing opulently instead of stingily, when you learn to think without limits, refusing to be cramped by your own limiting thoughts, you will find that the thing that you are seeking is seeking you and will meet you halfway.

Do not apologize when lack decides to show

up in your life or continuously confess your lack of this or that. Every time you confirm that you have nothing fit to wear, that you never have things that other people have, that you never go anywhere or do things that other people do, you are simply etching this sad picture deeper and deeper into your subconscious mind. As long as you recite these unfortunate details and dwell upon your disagreeable experiences, your mentality will not attract the thing you desire nor that which will remedy your difficult conditions.

Prosperity begins in the mind and is impossible to manifest in your life with a mental attitude that is hostile to it. Your mental picture must correspond to the reality that you seek. You cannot attract opulence if you are driven by a poverty-stricken attitude and mentality. It is fatal to work for one thing and expect something else. No matter how much one may long for prosperity, a miserable, poverty-stricken mental attitude will close all avenues to it. The weaving of the web is bound to follow the pattern. Opulence and prosperity cannot come through poverty thoughts and failing thought channels. Prosperity is created first in the mind, then it will appear in your natural experience.

Many people live with the belief that there is plenty of good things in this world for others (comforts, luxuries, beautiful houses, fine clothing, the opportunity for travel, leisure), but just not for them. They settle into and accept the conviction that these things do not belong to them but are for a different class of people. But why are they in a different class? Simply put, they think themselves into a different class and into a place of inferiority. They place limits on themselves and accept the lie that "those things" are not for them.

Thoughts of inferiority, lack, and limitation cause you to erect bars between you and plenty. You cut off the flow of abundance to you and make the law of supply inoperable in your life by shutting your mind to it. By what law can you expect to get what you believe you cannot have? By what philosophy can you obtain the good things of the world when you are thoroughly convinced that they are not for you?

Limitation is in man, not in the Creator. The Father wants His children to have all of the good things of the universe because He has fashioned them for His own. If you do not allow the good of God to flow to you, you limit yourself.

One of the greatest curses of the world is to believe in the necessity of poverty. Many people have a strong conviction that some people were born to be poor. However, there was no poverty, no want and no lack in the Creator's plan for Man. There should not be a poor person on the planet. The earth is full of resources which we have secretly, yet scarcely touched. It is as if someone is keeping it a big secret.

People are poor in the very midst of abundance simply because of their own limiting thoughts. Thoughts are things and are incorporated into life's abundance. If we are afraid of poverty and experiencing want, the poverty thoughts and fear thoughts are incorporated into our life texture and make us the magnet that attracts more poverty like itself. It was never intended for us to have such a difficult time making a living, to manage to just squeeze by to get a few more comforts, to spend all of our life making a living instead of making a life. The abundant life, full, free and beautiful was intended for us. If we were absolutely normal, our living getting would be a mere incident to our life-making.

The great ambition of the human race should be to develop a superb type of manhood, a beautiful, magnificent womanhood, man making, man building, instead of dollar making, as we see now. Resolve that you will turn your back on the poverty mentality, vigorously expect prosperity and hold tenaciously to the thought of abundance, the opulent idea which is befitting your nature, and live in the realization of plenty to actually feel rich. This will help you to attain that which you long for.

Confidence in the Source

There is a creative force and an intense desire for prosperity and abundance. The fact is we live in our own worlds. We are creations of our own thoughts. Each person builds his own world by his thought habit. You have the choice to dwell in an atmosphere of abundance or lack, plenty or want. However, God's children were not made to grovel. We were created to aspire, to prosper, to have dominion, to look up, not down. We were not made to pinch along in poverty, but we were made to acquire larger, grander things.

Nothing is too good for the children of the Prince of Peace. Nothing is too beautiful for the sons and daughters of God. Nothing is too grand, too sublime, too magnificent for us to enjoy. It is the poverty attitude and the narrowness of our thoughts that limit us. If we had a larger, grander conception of life and our birthright, if instead of whining, crawling, grumbling, sneaking and apologizing, we were to stand erect and claim our kingship and demand our rightful inheritance, the inheritance which is an abundance of all that is good and beautiful and true, we would live far more complete and fuller lives. As heirs of God we should not be so poverty-stricken. However, the narrowness of our faith and our misconception of our true birthright causes many to miss their divine inheritance and walk in the fullness of abundance and unlimited supply.

There is vast evidence in our construction and environment that proves that Man was made for infinitely grander and superb things that seemingly only the most fortunate possess and enjoy. Why not expect great, grand things if we are made in God's image and we are His children? We are heirs of all that He is, all that He has and all that is beautiful and opulent in the universe. Those who expect and appreciate the wealth of God will have access to obtain it.

There is something wrong when the sons and daughters of the King of kings, those who have inherited all the good things of the universe and live on the very shores plenty unspeakable, choose to walk past the very doors that house their infinite supply. Our circumstances in life, our financial conditions, our poverty or wealth, our friends or lack thereof are the offspring of our thoughts. If your mental attitude has been one of want and you have meditated heavily on thoughts of want and lack, your environment will correspond.

However, if your thinking has been open, generous and broad? If you have thoughts of abundance and prosperity and have made a relative effort to realize these conditions in your life, your environment will correspond. Everything we get in life comes through the gateway of our thoughts and resembles the quality of our thoughts. If our thoughts are pinching, stingy and mean, we will see that in our natural experience.

When we see people who for years have been in a poverty-stricken condition, unless they have suffered ill health or some unusual misfortune, we know that they have been in sin, the sin of harbouring the wrong mental attitude. Look to the head of the house, and you will find a complainer against the fate of his supply and one who believes in the smallness of his inflow. If you are dissatisfied with your condition, if you feel that life has been hard and fate cruel, if you are a complainer of your lot, you will probably find that whatever your condition may be in your home, business or social life it is the legitimate offspring of your own thoughts, ideas, and beliefs. You have no one to blame but you.

Right thinking will produce right living, clean thinking a clean life, and prosperous, generous thoughts followed by the intelligent endeavour to make your thoughts and your ideals real will produce corresponding results. If we learn to implicitly trust the great dispenser of all good, the Source of infinite supply, the power which brings seedtime and harvests, the power which generates our supply, the power which bids us no thought for tomorrow but considers the lilies how they grow and how they live best to improve the conditions, we shall never know want.

The human race lacks the unquestioned, implicit confidence in the Divine Source of all supply. As heirs of God we should stand in relation to the Infinite Source, as the child does to his parents. The child does not say, "I dare not eat this food for fear I may not get any more." He takes everything with absolute confidence and assurance that all of his needs will be supplied and that there is plenty more in the storehouse.

God intended for us to live the abundant life and to have plenty of everything that is good. However, many people are not aware of their possibilities. They do not expect enough of themselves. They do not demand enough - hence the meagerness and the stinginess of what they actually receive in life. They do not demand the abundance that rightfully belongs to them - hence the leanness, the lack of fullness and the incompleteness of their lives. They do not demand the royalty that is due to them. They are content with too little of the things worthwhile.

No one was meant to live in poverty and wretchedness. The lack of anything that is desirable is not natural to the constitution of any human being. Hold the thought that you are one with what you want. Be so in tune with it that you attract it. Keep your mind vigorously concentrated upon it. Never doubt your ability to get what you desire, and you will see the manifestation thereof in your world. Poverty is a mental disease. If you are suffering from it and are a victim of it, you will be surprised to see how quickly your condition will improve when you change your mental attitude: Instead of holding that miserable, shivering, limited poverty image, turnabout and face towards abundance, plenty, freedom, and happiness.

Success comes through a perfectly scientific mental process. The man who becomes prosperous believes he is going to be prosperous. He has faith in his ability to make money. He does not start out with his mind filled with doubt and fear. He does not constantly engage in poverty conversations. He does not think poverty thoughts. He does not live like a pauper. Instead, he turns his face towards the thing he is striving for, he is determined to get it, and he will not admit any contrary picture in his mind.

There are multitudes of poor people in this world who are satisfied with remaining in poverty and who have ceased to make a desperate struggle to rise out of it. They may work hard, but they have lost hope and expectation of being free from poverty's clutches. Many people keep themselves poor because they have an intense fear of poverty, allowing themselves to dwell upon the possibility of falling into a state of want and lack and dwelling upon conditions of poverty. The minds of children in many families are saturated with poverty thoughts. They hear conversations of poverty, lack, and limitation from morning till night. They see poverty-stricken conditions everywhere. Everything around them suggests poverty. Is it no wonder, that children brought up in such an atmosphere repeat the same poverty-stricken conditions of their parents and environment.

Fear of poverty, constant worry about making ends meet and fear of an awful, rainy day not only makes you unhappy, but you are adding to a load which is already too heavy for you to bear. No matter how bleak the outlook or how barren your environment, positively refuse to see anything that is unfavourable. Positively refuse to see any condition that intends to enslave you and keep you from expressing the best that you are. Positively refuse to do it and see what happens in your life.

God is Truth

God's word is true. However, many people try to conceal the main purpose of their lives. They tell all kinds of stories about what they are seeking. Often they confess that all they have is enough to feed, clothe and house their families. Many confess, "I don't want too much." That kind of thinking is not of God. That is not your truth. Those are your thoughts, not the thoughts of God.

Be honest about your pursuit of God's unlimited bounty because that is what God has intended for you. Nothing can satisfy short of unlimited supply, for God is unlimited supply. God is the very idea of unlimited supply which Man keeps suppressed within his mind. Name your good. Confess your good. Declare your good. Do not fail to say, *"My good is unlimited support,"* and you will see that good soon bring you marvellous support. New provisions will be made for you.

There is no limit to the bounty of truth. Any thoughts contrary to this truth are not the God-in-you speaking. That is the human you limiting God. God's truth is unlimited supply. The substance of truth is shown by the prosperity that is sure to come to you when you speak the truth. Jesus said that all who learn his doctrine will receive a hundredfold more possessions in their life. We are told by Jesus to take no thought for ourselves, to sit down and proclaim to the universe, *"My support is my God. My good is my God. God is my support."*

Stop muzzling God. Jesus said that in this life we will have tribulation while getting our good support, but He also said, *"Be not afraid, I have overcome."* (John 16:33) This is His word. He meant he has overcome the worldly ways of being supported by telling the truth and that good will surely come to you. Tribulation is the opposition that we meet by telling the world that we get our support by thinking and speaking the truth. Tribulation is the feeling we have when we first set forth as grown men and women into the way which is exactly opposite to a former way of thinking. It is tribulation to attempt to cast away all anxiety. It is tribulation to give up trying to obtain our living through our old mind.

Every time God deposits a truth in you, whether it comes through the Spirit of God within you, whether it comes through a prophetic word or whether it comes through a child, immediately as that truth is deposited you will encounter tribulation. You will hear your truth that you are healed and right away you will get tribulation. Know that that is the way of life, but it must not move you off course. It must not sway you from your truth. The only way to get God's truth is to speak it.

"In the beginning was the Word, and the Word was with God, and the Word was God." (John 1:1)

You have to speak His truth. Good is God. God is substance. God is Spirit. Therefore, your supply comes from Spirit and as Spirit. It is not tribulation to practice providing for you by telling the truth. After a little while, you wouldn't have the tribulation because you will know exactly how Spirit works. But right now, every time a truth is deposited in you, you look to materiality to support a spiritual truth. The two do not mix. Receive your truth and eventually, you will see it in material form. But first, you have to receive it. Many people fall into the trap of doubt before they receive it and as a result, do not speak it. They keep it silent and focus on the tribulation. Erroneously, they voice the tribulation. However, when you constantly focus on the tribulation you are declaring that God's word will not come to pass. However, you never gave it a chance. You never spoke it. You never recognized it.

Love, life, truth, substance, intelligence are names of our good. Declare that your good is truth. This will cause your lips to speak the truth. There is no evil in good. God is good. So, there is no evil in God. There is no evil in God, and there is no evil in His goodness. When you speak your truth and mix it with evil, it is no longer your truth. It is something else that you are speaking. When God gives you a word, when God gives you the truth hold on to it!

As soon as we say, *"God is not the author of*

sickness; God is good; good is truth; truth is God," we are brought to the place where we can no longer declare that sickness is good. Good is God, therefore, God is health. It is well to say that God is unbounded, unlimited love. God is our love. There is an instinctive seeking of all things for love. When you say that God is love that is where you will be guided. Many dying men have been saved by feeling their mother's soft kiss on their forehead. Many women have lifted their dying face and lived when the voice of their children heard them calling their name.

My mother had Alzheimer's and the doctors were counting down the days. She was unable to recognize anyone. I went to see her. They kept telling her, "It's your daughter, Gloria." I said, "It's Gloria." Finally, something got through and she said, "My Gloria?" And with that, there was an awakening.

Do not underestimate the power of love. God is love. God is truth. Love is truth. Declare your truth, *"The good I am seeking is love."* The heights and depths and splendour of love have not been told. God's love is so great that it was personified through His son Jesus. The little children came close to his knees, poor, neglected women followed him, the blind and the beggars clung to His clothes, and dignitaries came by night to speak with Him. Love does not come to us by any one man, woman or child and then goes away. That is only a sign of love. God's love is eternal. God's love is infinite.

"For I know the thoughts that I think toward you, saith the LORD, thoughts of

peace, and not of evil, to give you an expected end." (Jeremiah 29:11)

How shall we attain our good? We cannot attain our good by working with our hands for countless ages. We can only attain the fullness of God's good for our lives through the way of Jesus Christ. Jesus Christ is all truth. The Jesus Christ method brings the fulfillment of all experience. You must expect the good of God to overflow in your life and be very definite and assured that you will see it manifest in your life. Have a clear idea of a sweet, free and unburdened life. Visualize it. See it in your mind's eye. If you have a clear idea of the picture in your mind, you will be able to focus on the God within you and bring that life forward. However, you have to create it in your mind first. You have to picture it and declare very plainly, *"This sweet, free, unburdened life*

IS my good."

Do not be afraid to claim your truth. Do not be afraid to claim your good. If health is part of your good, have a clear idea of how sweet and joyous health will feel. Name it as the name of your good. When you have a clear idea of your good, you will find that your good will come and settle upon you. It will sift itself through you. It can burst forward in your life by the little sounds in your system. Jesus said, *"The meek shall inherit the earth."* (Matthew 5:5) Let it be in your mouth also. Be definite when you give this statement of good, which is the statement of your being. Expect to see it work quickly in your life. Truth is not slow. Truth is quick. Truth it now!

"(For he saith, I have heard thee in a time accepted, and in the day of salvation have I

succoured thee: behold, now is the accepted time; behold, now is the day of salvation.)" (2 Corinthians 6:2)

Jesus said, *"Now is the accepted time."* Truth does not have to make things new for you. In truth, it was so from the beginning. *"All truth is waiting for you to plainly declare your Good."* This speaking out and declaring continuously what we have felt intuitive is the first movement towards demonstration, manifestation, and satisfaction. You have to declare your truth. Do not be afraid. Do not let outside circumstances stop you from declaring your truth. Know that God is your Source and that He is the Infinite Source. Any time you start limiting God know that it is your humanness that is limiting you, it is not your truth. Declare your truth, and you will see it unfold in your life.

Continually declare, *"The good that I am seeking is my God."* Now, that good could be anything. It could be prosperity. It could be health. It could be joy. It could be a loving relationship. If you mix any kind of dis-ease with your truth, know that it is not God. Any time doubt tries to creep in, go back to the truth that God has deposited in your heart and declare it. Keep your eyes on it. Hold steadfast to it. If God put it in you, it is because it is already decreed for you to have it. It is already available to you. It is yours. Your Father wants to give you the kingdom!

"Fear not, little flock; for it is your Father's good pleasure to give you the kingdom. (Luke 12:32)

AFFIRMATION:

Now, declare this affirmation of your Good and expect God to deliver...

"The good I am seeking is my God. God is my life. The good I am seeking is my health. God is my health. The good I am seeking is my strength. God is my strength. The good I am seeking is my support. God is my support. The good I am seeking is my defence. God is my defence. Life is God. Truth is God. Love is God. Substance is God. God is intelligence omnipresent, omnipotent, omniscience. God is life omnipresent, omnipotent, omniscience. God is truth, omnipresent, omnipotent, omniscience. God is love omnipresent, omnipotent, omniscience. God is Spirit omnipresent, omnipotent, omniscience.

God is truth."

CHAPTER 11

THERE IS NONE OF THY KINDRED THAT IS LED BY THIS NAME

Now Elisabeth's full time came that she should be delivered; and she brought forth a son. And her neighbours and her cousins heard how the Lord had shewed great mercy upon her; and they rejoiced with her. And it came to pass, that on the eighth day they came to circumcise the child; and they called him Zacharias, after the name of his father. And his mother answered and said, Not so; but he shall be called John. And they said unto her, there is none of thy kindred that is called by this name. And they made signs to his father, how he would have him called. And he asked for a writing table, and wrote, saying, His name is John. And they marvelled all. And his mouth was opened immediately, and his tongue loosed, and he spake, and praised God. And fear came on all that dwelt round about them: and all these sayings were noised abroad throughout all the hill country of Judaea. And all they that heard them laid them up in their hearts, saying, What manner of child shall this be! And the hand of the Lord was with him. Luke 1:57-66

Before we begin I want to take you back a bit at the beginning of the scripture from verse 11 when they were all praying:

And there appeared unto him an angel of the Lord standing on the right side of the altar of incense. And when Zacharias saw him, *he was troubled, and fear fell upon him. But the angel said unto him, Fear not, Zacharias: for thy prayer is heard; and thy wife Elisabeth shall bear thee a son, and thou shalt call his name John. And thou shalt have joy and gladness; and many shall rejoice at his birth. For he shall be great in the sight of the Lord, and shall drink neither wine nor strong drink; and he shall be filled with the Holy Ghost, even from his mother's womb. And many of the children of Israel shall he turn to the Lord their God. And he shall go before him in the spirit and power of Elias, to turn the hearts of the fathers to the children, and the disobedient to the wisdom of the just; to make ready a people prepared for the Lord. And Zacharias said unto the angel, Whereby shall I know this? for I am an old man, and my wife well stricken in years. And the angel answering said unto him, I am Gabriel, that stand in the presence of God; and am sent to speak unto thee, and to shew thee these glad tidings. And, behold, thou shalt be dumb, and not able to speak, until the day that these things shall be performed, because thou believest not my words, which shall be fulfilled in their season. And the people waited for Zacharias, and marvelled that he tarried so long in the temple. And when he came out, he could not speak unto them: and they perceived that he had seen a vision in the temple: for he beckoned unto them, and remained speechless.*

We all came into this world with a set of values, norms, and traditions set out for us. We did not have a hand in establishing what language we were going to speak, that was already chosen; We did not have a hand in the environment we were going to grow up in; That was already establish: We did not have a hand in the type of food we were going to eat; That too was establish. You did not have a say in your chosen religion for that too was establish.

So, you came into this world with a number of decisions already establish for you along with societies expectation that you would follow your pre-disdained path: You believed what was told to you, and it formed part of your belief system which ended up guiding your path. As you grow and develop you come to the realization that the norm that was established for you is conflicting with your view on life. For example, everyone in your family was farmers, but you want to be an engineer: Young girls were taught sewing, but you want to be a teacher; You are part of a family of doctors, but you want to be a lawyer.

These types of conflicts are not new, however; it does not make them less challenging. So you fight with everyone for a space to express yourself: By so doing causing yourself and others a tremendous amount of pain: Could I tell you that the real battle is not with the people around you but with yourself! In essence, you are bucking up against your own belief system.

Change can be painful in the absence of inner acceptance. If you do not accept the fact that you are not cut out to be a farmer, and are still trying your hand at it in order to please your family how do you expect to succeed? You cannot succeed if your heart is not in it. Succeed demands a 100% commitment.

So, an angel told Elisabeth that she was going to have a son and to call him John. Now we all know what Angels are: They are ministering spirits, in essence, they are those good productive thoughts that guide you through a situation: So, the thought of having a baby came to her and she believed so it is established in her. However, there is another voice around her who is an unbeliever.

What do you do when you have an idea that

feels right inside you, but everyone around you is opposed to it? I will tell you what you do. You keep that thing close to your chest and tell no one until it comes to term. If you talk too soon, you could abort the whole God-given idea. This was the case with Elisabeth, she was surrounded by unbelief. She had to shut that thing up until she came to term.

Remember this: *And the angel answering said unto him, I am Gabriel, that stand in the presence of God; and am sent to speak unto thee, and to shew thee these glad tidings. And, behold, thou shalt be dumb, and not able to speak, until the day that these things shall be performed, because thou believest not my words, which shall be fulfilled in their season. And the people waited for Zacharias, and marvelled that he tarried so long in the temple. And when he came out, he could not speak unto them: and they perceived that he had seen a vision in the temple: for he beckoned unto them, and remained speechless.*

Sometimes in life, you have to shut up the doubting Thomas. However, you cannot shut them up outside of yourself. You have to shut them up from the inside. This is a real battle! You cannot change anybody. And nobody can change you. The work is completed in the individual. You can only change yourselves and in so doing you would see that new self in the people you meet.

Having said all that, I want you to know this! Very little progress can be made on the spiritual path of life until we have caught some vision of what God is, of what our relationship to God is, and of what God's function is in our life. This cannot be a vicarious experience; it must be individual and it must be approached in a complete relax manner. We must be unwilling to accept any authority other than our own interior revelation. So we ask ourselves questions about God, which will lead into a meditation on God: What is God? What does God mean to me? What is the place and function of God in my life?

How many people have ever had a God-experience? How many have felt the flow of the Spirit in their minds, in their souls, in their bodies? The number is small, only a few hundred or at the most a few thousand in a generation; and yet God is available to every man, woman, and child. God demands our entire love and devotion; we must give ourselves to Him so that He may reveal the eternal giving-ness of Himself to us. We must love God supremely with our whole heart, mind, and soul; love God so much that our only prayer is: I Must Feel

God; I must Let God fill my soul, my heart, my mind, my being, my very body.

We speak of God as impersonal Intelligence, Mind, Principle, But God is personal too. Could I tell you that the relationship between an individual and God is closer than his relationship with his mother? It is like reaching out and feeling a presence always there, gentle, reassuring in its very quietness; it is joy, peace, and warmth. The moment we have a God-experience that gentleness is there, that peace is there, that warmth is there, and with it comes love toward everything in this world, a sense of companionship and joy in one another.

Now! The normal concept of God is that of a God separate and apart from us, who has within Himself all good, but is withholding it from us. Usually, in praying to God, it is for a purpose of seeking or getting something from God; health, supply, opportunity, companionship. Most of us believe that God possesses this good, but for some inexplicable reason is withholding it from us, and so we pray to God to bestow some of it upon us. Sometimes, if our prayers are not answered quickly enough, we make all sorts of promises in futile attempt to bargain with God–promises which often we have no intention of keeping.

In a vain effort to reconcile a supposedly loving God with a God who turns a deaf ear to our supplications, we often censure ourselves, believing that some evil act of omission or commission is the reason God is withholding good from us. Some physicians content that many of the ills of the world, both mental and physical, are the result of guilt complexes.

Countless people live in a state of troubling self-condemnation, consumed by a sense of guilt; sometimes for some serious offence committed in their past; sometimes for some small or inconsequential act. If we believe that we are being punished by a vengeful God, our concept of God is entirely erroneous, because God has no memory of our faults and failings; God is too pure to behold inequity. God has not punished and does not punish sinners. The sinner is punished by his own sin, not by God. Even the confirmed sinner knows that there are certain laws of God which must not be violated. He knows that if he violates these laws, punishment follows, but what he does not know is that punishment is not God-inflicted, but self-inflicted.

God is not a vindictive God: God is not a withholding God, but neither is He a giving God. God is Love and He neither withholds nor punishes; there is no love in withholding and there is no love in punishment. If God waited for us to be good or deserving, if He waited for us to find the right words with which to soothe Him, if He waited for us to use a form of mediation which is pleasing in His eyes before He was willing to bestow His blessings upon us, He would be a cruel and capricious God. God will never give more than He is giving us now. God is forever being God: God is being Life; God is being love; and God is forever expressing Its life and Its love.

PASTOR DR. GLORIA TAYLOR-BOYCE

CHAPTER 12

THE GREAT COMMISSION

*Then the eleven disciples went away into Galilee, into a mountain where Jesus had appointed them. And when they saw him, they worshipped him: but some doubted. And Jesus came and spake unto them, saying, **ALL** power is given unto me in heaven and in earth. Go ye therefore, and teach **ALL** nations, baptizing them in the name of the Father, and of the Son, and of the Holy Ghost: Teaching them to observe **ALL** things whatsoever I have commanded you: and, lo, I am with you **ALWAYS,** even unto the end of the world. Amen.*
MATTHEW 28:16-20

Today's gospel taken from Matthew 28: 16-20, is known as **THE GREAT COMMISSION:** The arrest and crucifixion of Jesus was a deeply disorienting experience for his followers, ruthlessly dashing in a matter of hours the great hopes and dreams they all shared.

They had lost one they loved and admired to a vicious execution. Now, to see Jesus alive after his death, which they naturally assumed had ended everything, must have been utterly astonishing. Nothing in their history or Jewish faith had prepared them for what was occurring. To say they struggled with cognitive conflict would be an understatement.

Matthew 28.16-20 provides the narrative of the last recorded encounter of Jesus by the disciples and the final words of Jesus close the Gospel. Directed to return to Galilee where Jesus would meet up with them, the disciples followed yet again, not knowing what they would encounter. Galilee was where it all began and Galilee, it seems, would mark the new beginning.

It is difficult to imagine what their journey was like, but it had to have been a memorable one. It was the ultimate road trip, filled with long conversations that focused upon making sense of the mind-bending events that had transpired, wondering aloud what would happen next. This moment with Jesus would be an important time for them. They had lost everything in the disastrous events that preceded this, and they were on their way to discover what, if anything would be next.

We all struggle to comprehend the

astonishing work of God in Christ. Having reunited with Jesus in Galilee, the disciples' response is somewhat peculiar. Upon seeing Jesus, they worship. This part we understand; it makes sense given the circumstances of Jesus' resurrection and the preceding events. But they also **doubt.** Worship is not typically associated with doubt. In fact, many feel that even if they do doubt, they cannot admit it.

The passage here does not so much focus on doubt in the sense of unbelief as it does on the cognitive conflict that arises from unusual, even unbelievable, circumstances. This is one case where the understanding of the world and the way that God had previously worked in it did not match with what they saw before them.

Jesus' parting words are commonly referred

to as the Great Commission. But it is more than that; the reference of the text is much broader. The text frames the basis for the communal identity and life together for the movement that will become the church. Four elements emerge that draw our attention.

There are four "alls" in Today's Gospel: Jesus has **all** authority given to him, we are to make disciples of **all** nations, we are to teach that we should obey **all** that he commanded during his earthly life, and the promise that closes, is that he will be with us **always**. These four "alls" capture much of what the paragraph intends to communicate and also the central message of the Gospel of Matthew.

All authority: The incarnation and Jesus' life on earth were marked by his profound humanity. Apart from a glimpse of his glory during the Transfiguration, this is a Jesus we are not accustomed to. In this scene the authority that Jesus taught with and exercised in his healings and deliverances becomes positional. He has been given all authority in heaven and on earth, and the disciples' teacher is now revealed as the Lord of all. The power of passages like Matthew 11:25-30 reside in the person of Jesus. Similarly, the commission that follows has little authority if Jesus were not the Son of God.

All nations: The purpose of God is to be reconciled with all humanity, which includes every nationality and race. Jesus' ministry was primarily limited to the Jewish people throughout Matthew's gospel, but here the boundaries are now expanded to include all humanity. Thus the commission has an international scope. Note, however, that the text does not say to take the *gospel* to the nations, although it is implied. Jesus here actually says that they are to *make disciples* of all nations. This is the primary verb of the section, and it is a command.

Superficial evangelism is not Jesus' intent; rather, Jesus has in mind a task that is more robust. The disciples are students. In this case, they are, like the twelve disciples in the gospel narrative, to become devoted followers of Jesus and together live out his teachings within the broader society. Further, they are to baptize in the name of the Trinity. This baptism becomes the start of a ritual that symbolically marks the movement from death to life.

All that he commanded: Of all the gospels, Matthew's is the most teaching oriented. Matthew structures his gospel in such a way that he includes five major sections of Jesus' teachings. The third part of the command is to teach those who become disciples to do everything that Jesus commanded. This follows Jesus' own instructions in Matthew 5:16 and Matthew 7:21-27, in which he underlines the necessity of doing what he teaches and not merely paying lip service. Our actions should reflect our beliefs. Statements of faith are important within communities, but Matthew reminds us that faith without appropriate behaviour is empty.

Always with us: Matthew closes with what is perhaps one of the most comforting statements in Scripture. Jesus, as Lord of all, promises to be with us, the church, always, even until the final consummation of everything. This continuing, abiding presence of Jesus is a profound promise. The gospel opens with a similar affirmation in Matthew1:23, in which Jesus is named Emmanuel or "God with us." This ending reminds us of the person of Jesus in his earthly life--the one who shared space with people, lived and was present with them and showed us what God is like.

The scripture moves us from the disciples' insecurity and lack of understanding to focus us on the exalted Lord, who as the leader of the movement defines reality. The commission is for all who are part of the people of God and incorporates the task of making disciples with teaching and baptizing as the movement expands around the world. The church is at its core to be living out the teachings of Jesus as a witness within their world. And perhaps most profoundly of all, Jesus promises that his presence will be with his people until the final conclusion of the ages.

In closing I am asking you to let us learn to see as God must, with a Perfect Vision. Let us seek the good and the true and believe in them with our whole heart, even though every man we meet is filled with suffering: and limitation appears at all sides. **We cannot afford to believe in imperfection for a single second**, to do so is to doubt God, to believe in another Creator. Let us daily say to ourselves: "Perfect God within me, Perfect Life within me, which is God, come forth into expression through me as that which I am; lead me ever into the paths of perfection and cause me to see only the Good." By this practice, the soul will become illumined and will acquaint itself with God and be at peace. "Be ye therefore perfect even as your

Father which is in heaven is perfect."

ABOUT SAINT ZOE PARISH CHURCH

Saint Zoe Parish Church is an independent church ministry established in November 2007 to minister to communities, families, and individuals.

A *not-for-profit* Christian Prophetic Church Ministry, it received Canadian Charitable status in 2009 under the guidance of Senior Pastor and Overseer, Pastor Dr. Ralph H. Boyce.

In January 2016, **Saint Zoe Parish Church** formed an alliance with the *Old Holy Catholic Church (O.H.C.C.)* which is *not Roman Catholic* to serve the Parish of Saint Zoe in the Brampton/Toronto Area. His Eminence, Archbishop Renair Laufers, is the covering Bishop for this ministry

We believe there is but one Lord and one baptism and embrace the Holy Scriptures.

SUNDAY WORSHIP MASS / SERVICE

Time: 12:30 PM – 1:30 PM EST

Location:

156 Main St. N, Brampton, On. **In the Historical Church Building at the Corner of **Church St.** & **Highway 10** ** Next to the 7/11 Store

Come! Celebrate and receive a Blessing! All are welcome!

LOCAL WEEKLY CHURCH SERVICES

In conjunction to the *Worship Services, Prayer Meetings* and other *Spiritual Enlightenment classes* which are run out of the local church facilities, there are many Conference Calls and Certificate programs which are conducted daily Online by Phone.

The Main Conference Call number is:

- 1-515-604-9300 Access Code: 425747#

- **1-425-426-1290** next **515-604-9300#** access code **425747#** If you are having a challenge

OTHER METHODS TO CONNECT:
Cellphone or Tablet

Download the FreeConferenceCall APP to your phone and connected to WiFi:

- Meeting ID: zoecanada

- Select the Internet option

- Click the phone icon from the dropdown menu click the speaker icon

- Mute and unMute by Clicking on the Microphone icon at the lower left of your screen

On your computer:

- Click this link:

www.freeconferencecall.com/join/zoecanada

Any questions call Pastor Dr. Ralph Boyce toll-free at 1-800-441-0239 ext 2 or 1-905-451-3111

NOTES

Made in the USA
Columbia, SC
05 August 2018